State of Exception

State of Exception ℵ *Giorgio Agamben*

TRANSLATED BY KEVIN ATTELL

THE UNIVERSITY OF CHICAGO PRESS

Chicago and London

GIORGIO AGAMBEN is professor of aesthetics at the University of Verona. He is the author of ten previous books, including the prequel to this one, *Homo Sacer: Sovereign Power and Bare Life,* published in English by Stanford University Press.

KEVIN ATTELL is a postdoctoral fellow in the English Department at the University of California, Davis. He is the translator of Giorgio Agamben's *The Open: Man and Animal.*

The University of Chicago Press, Chicago 60637
The University of Chicago Press, Ltd., London
© 2005 by The University of Chicago
All rights reserved. Published 2005
Printed in the United States of America

14 13 12 11 10 09 08 07 06 05   1 2 3 4 5

ISBN (cloth): 0-226-00924-6
ISBN (paper): 0-226-00925-4

Originally published as *Stato di eccezione,* © 2003 Bollati Boringhieri editore s.r.l., Torino.

Library of Congress Cataloging-in-Publication Data

Agamben, Giorgio, 1942–
    [Stato di eccezione. English]
    State of exception / Giorgio Agamben ; translated by Kevin Attell.
        p.   cm.
    Includes bibliographical references (p.   ) and index.
    ISBN 0-226-00924-6 (cloth : alk. paper) — ISBN 0-226-00925-4 (pbk. : alk. paper)
        1. War and emergency powers.   2. State of siege.   3. War and emergency powers—Europe—History.   4. War and emergency powers—United States—History.   5. State of siege—Europe—History.   6. State of siege—United States—History.   I. Title.
        JF256.A3413   2005
        321—dc22   2004013680

⊗ The paper used in this publication meets the minimum requirements of the American National Standard for Information Sciences—Permanence of Paper for Printed Library Materials, ANSI Z39.48-1992.

Contents

Translator's Note

Wherever possible, I have included references to published English translations of Agamben's French, German, and Italian sources in the references list. However, in order to maintain consistency in terminology throughout the text, and to better reflect Agamben's own translations of these sources, the published English versions have frequently been modified. Where an English edition is listed in the bibliography, the first page number in the text citation refers to the original, and the second to the English edition (e.g., [Benjamin 1942, 697/257]). Where no English edition is listed, the translation is mine.

I would like to give my deepest thanks to Courtney Booker, David Copenhafer, Samuel Gilbert, Sirietta Simoncini, and to Giorgio Agamben for their generous help in preparing this translation.

Quare siletis juristae in munere vestro?

[Why are you jurists silent about that which concerns you?]

1 ℵ The State of Exception as a Paradigm of Government

1.1   The essential contiguity between the state of exception and sovereignty was established by Carl Schmitt in his book *Politische Theologie* (1922). Although his famous definition of the sovereign as "he who
decides on the state of exception" has been widely commented on and
discussed, there is still no theory of the state of exception in public law,
and jurists and theorists of public law seem to regard the problem more
as a *quaestio facti* than as a genuine juridical problem. Not only is such
a theory deemed illegitimate by those authors who (following the ancient maxim according to which *necessitas legem non habet* [necessity
has no law]) affirm that the state of necessity, on which the exception
is founded, cannot have a juridical form, but it is difficult even to arrive at a definition of the term given its position at the limit between
politics and law. Indeed, according to a widely held opinion, the state
of exception constitutes a "point of imbalance between public law and
political fact" (Saint-Bonnet 2001, 28) that is situated—like civil war,
insurrection and resistance—in an "ambiguous, uncertain, borderline
fringe, at the intersection of the legal and the political" (Fontana 1999,
16). The question of borders becomes all the more urgent: if exceptional
measures are the result of periods of political crisis and, as such, must
be understood on political and not juridico-constitutional grounds (De
Martino 1973, 320), then they find themselves in the paradoxical position
of being juridical measures that cannot be understood in legal terms,
and the state of exception appears as the legal form of what cannot have
legal form. On the other hand, if the law employs the exception—that
is the suspension of law itself—as its original means of referring to and
encompassing life, then a theory of the state of exception is the prelim-
inary condition for any definition of the relation that binds and, at the
same time, abandons the living being to law.

It is this no-man's-land between public law and political fact, and
between the juridical order and life, that the present study seeks to

investigate. Only if the veil covering this ambiguous zone is lifted will we be able to approach an understanding of the stakes involved in the difference—or the supposed difference—between the political and the juridical, and between law and the living being. And perhaps only then will it be possible to answer the question that never ceases to reverberate in the history of Western politics: what does it mean to act politically?

1.2   One of the elements that make the state of exception so difficult to define is certainly its close relationship to civil war, insurrection, and resistance. Because civil war is the opposite of normal conditions, it lies in a zone of undecidability with respect to the state of exception, which is state power's immediate response to the most extreme internal conflicts. Thus, over the course of the twentieth century, we have been able to witness a paradoxical phenomenon that has been effectively defined as a "legal civil war" (Schnur 1983). Let us take the case of the Nazi State. No sooner did Hitler take power (or, as we should perhaps more accurately say, no sooner was power given to him) than, on February 28, he proclaimed the Decree for the Protection of the People and the State, which suspended the articles of the Weimar Constitution concerning personal liberties. The decree was never repealed, so that from a juridical standpoint the entire Third Reich can be considered a state of exception that lasted twelve years. In this sense, modern totalitarianism can be defined as the establishment, by means of the state of exception, of a legal civil war that allows for the physical elimination not only of political adversaries but of entire categories of citizens who for some reason cannot be integrated into the political system. Since then, the voluntary creation of a permanent state of emergency (though perhaps not declared in the technical sense) has become one of the essential practices of contemporary states, including so-called democratic ones.

Faced with the unstoppable progression of what has been called a "global civil war," the state of exception tends increasingly to appear as the dominant paradigm of government in contemporary politics. This transformation of a provisional and exceptional measure into a technique of government threatens radically to alter—in fact, has already palpably altered—the structure and meaning of the traditional distinction between constitutional forms. Indeed, from this perspective, the state of exception appears as a threshold of indeterminacy between democracy and absolutism.

א The expression "global civil war" appears in the same year (1963) in both Hannah Arendt's *On Revolution* and Carl Schmitt's *Theory of the Partisan*. However, as we will see, the distinction between a "real state of exception" (*état de siège effectif*) and a "fictitious state of exception" (*état de siège fictif*) goes back to French public law theory and was already clearly articulated in Theodor Reinach's book *De l'état de siège. Étude historique et juridique* (1885), which is at the origins of the Schmittian and Benjaminian opposition between a real and a fictitious state of exception. Anglo-Saxon jurisprudence prefers to speak here of "fancied emergency." For their part, Nazi jurists spoke openly of a *gewollte Ausnahmezustand*, a "willed state of exception," "for the sake of establishing the National Socialist State" (Werner Spohr, quoted in Drobische and Wieland 1993, 28).

1.3   The immediately biopolitical significance of the state of exception as the original structure in which law encompasses living beings by means of its own suspension emerges clearly in the "military order" issued by the president of the United States on November 13, 2001, which authorized the "indefinite detention" and trial by "military commissions" (not to be confused with the military tribunals provided for by the law of war) of noncitizens suspected of involvement in terrorist activities.

The USA Patriot Act issued by the U.S. Senate on October 26, 2001, already allowed the attorney general to "take into custody" any alien suspected of activities that endangered "the national security of the United States," but within seven days the alien had to be either released or charged with the violation of immigration laws or some other criminal offense. What is new about President Bush's order is that it radically erases any legal status of the individual, thus producing a legally unnamable and unclassifiable being. Not only do the Taliban captured in Afghanistan not enjoy the status of POWs as defined by the Geneva Convention, they do not even have the status of persons charged with a crime according to American laws. Neither prisoners nor persons accused, but simply "detainees," they are the object of a pure de facto rule, of a detention that is indefinite not only in the temporal sense but in its very nature as well, since it is entirely removed from the law and from judicial oversight. The only thing to which it could possibly be compared is the legal situation of the Jews in the Nazi *Lager* [camps], who, along with their citizenship, had lost every legal identity, but at least retained their identity as Jews. As Judith Butler has effectively shown, in the detainee at Guantánamo, bare life reaches its maximum indeterminacy.

1.4   The uncertainty of the concept is exactly matched by terminological uncertainty. The present study will use the syntagma *state of exception* as the technical term for the consistent set of legal phenomena that it seeks to define. This term, which is common in German theory (*Ausnahmezustand,* but also *Notstand,* "state of necessity"), is foreign to Italian and French theory, which prefer to speak of *emergency decrees* and *state of siege* (political or fictitious, *état de siège fictif*). In Anglo-Saxon theory, the terms *martial law* and *emergency powers* prevail.

If, as has been suggested, terminology is the properly poetic moment of thought, then terminological choices can never be neutral. In this sense, the choice of the term *state of exception* implies a position taken on both the nature of the phenomenon that we seek to investigate and the logic most suitable for understanding it. Though the notions of *state of siege* and *martial law* express a connection with the state of war that has been historically decisive and is present to this day, they nevertheless prove to be inadequate to define the proper structure of the phenomenon, and they must therefore be qualified as *political* or *fictitious,* terms that are themselves misleading in some ways. The state of exception is not a special kind of law (like the law of war); rather, insofar as it is a suspension of the juridical order itself, it defines law's threshold or limit concept.

א The history of the term *fictitious or political state of siege* is instructive in this regard. It goes back to the French doctrine that—in reference to Napoleon's decree of December 24, 1811—provided for the possibility of a state of siege that the emperor could declare whether or not a city was actually under attack or directly threatened by enemy forces, "whenever circumstances require giving more forces and more power to the military police, without it being necessary to put the place in a state of siege" (Reinach 1885, 109). The institution of the state of siege has its origin in the French Constituent Assembly's decree of July 8, 1791, which distinguished among *état de paix*, in which military authority and civil authority each acts in its own sphere; *état de guerre*, in which civil authority must act in concert with military authority; and *état de siège*, in which "all the functions entrusted to the civil authority for maintaining order and internal policing pass to the military commander, who exercises them under his exclusive responsibility" (ibid.). The decree referred only to military strongholds and ports, but with the law of 19 Fructidor Year 5, the Directory assimilated municipalities in the interior with the strongholds and, with the law of 18 Fructidor of the same year, granted itself the right to put a city in a state of siege. The subsequent history of the state of siege is the history of its gradual emancipation from the wartime situation to which it was originally bound in order to be used as an extraordinary police measure to cope with internal sedition and disorder, thus changing from a real, or military, state of siege to a fictitious, or political one. In any case, it is important not to forget that the modern state of exception is a creation of the democratic-revolutionary tradition and not the absolutist one.

The idea of a suspension of the constitution was introduced for the first time in the constitution of 22 Frimaire Year 8, Article 92 of which reads, "In the case of armed revolt or disturbances that would threaten the security of the State, the law can, in the places and for the time that it determines, suspend the rule of the constitution. In such cases, this suspension can be provisionally declared by a decree of the government if the legislative body is in recess, provided that this body be convened as soon as possible by an article of the same decree." The city or region in question was declared *hors la constitution*. Although the paradigm is, on the one hand (in the state of siege) the extension of the military authority's wartime powers into the civil sphere, and on the other a suspension of the constitution (or of those constitutional norms that protect individual liberties), in time the two models end up merging into a single juridical phenomenon that we call the *state of exception*.

א The expression *full powers (pleins pouvoirs)*, which is sometimes used to characterize the state of exception, refers to the expansion of the powers of the government, and in particular the conferral on the executive of the power to issue decrees having the force of law. It derives from the notion of *plenitudo potestatis*, which was elaborated in that true and proper laboratory of modern public legal terminology that was canon law. The presupposition here is that the state of exception entails a return to an original, pleromatic state in which the distinction among the different powers (legislative, executive, etc.) has not yet been produced. As we will see, the state of exception constitutes rather a kenomatic state, an emptiness of law, and the idea of an originary indistinction and fullness of power must be considered a legal mythologeme analogous to the idea of a state of nature (and it is not by chance that it was precisely Schmitt who had recourse to this mythologeme). In any case, the term *full powers* describes one of the executive power's possible modes of action during the state of exception, but it does not coincide with it.

1.5   Between 1934 and 1948, in the face of the collapse of Europe's democracies, the theory of the state of exception (which had made a first, isolated appearance in 1921 with Schmitt's book *Dictatorship*) saw a moment of particular fortune, but it is significant that this occurred in the pseudomorphic form of a debate over so-called constitutional dictatorship.

This term (which German jurists had already used to indicate the emergency [*eccezionali*] powers that Article 48 of the Weimar Constitution granted the president of the Reich [Hugo Preuss: *Reichsverfassungsmäßige Diktatur*]) was taken up again and developed by Frederick M. Watkins ("The Problem of Constitutional Dictatorship," 1940), Carl J. Friedrich (*Constitutional Government and Democracy*, [1941] 1950), and finally Clinton L. Rossiter (*Constitutional Dictatorship: Crisis Government in the Modern Democracies*, 1948). Before them, we must also at least mention the book by the Swedish jurist Herbert Tingsten, *Les pleins pouvoirs. L'expansion des pouvoirs gouvernementaux pendant et après la Grande Guerre* (1934). While these books are quite varied and as a whole more dependent on Schmitt's theory than a first reading might suggest, they are nevertheless equally important because they record for the first time how the democratic regimes were transformed by the gradual expansion of the executive's powers during the two world wars and, more generally, by the state of exception that had accompanied and followed those wars. They are in some ways the heralds who announced what we today have clearly before our eyes—namely, that since "the state of exception . . . has become the rule" (Benjamin 1942, 697/257), it not only appears increasingly as a technique of government rather than an exceptional measure, but it also lets its own nature as the constitutive paradigm of the juridical order come to light.

Tingsten's analysis centers on an essential technical problem that profoundly marks the evolution of the modern parliamentary regimes: the delegation contained in the "full powers" laws mentioned above, and the resulting extension of the executive's powers into the legislative sphere through the issuance of decrees and measures. "By 'full powers laws' we mean those laws by which an exceptionally broad regulatory power is granted to the executive, particularly the power to modify or abrogate by decree the laws in force" (Tingsten 1934, 13). Because laws of this nature, which should be issued to cope with exceptional circumstances of necessity or emergency, conflict with the fundamental hierarchy of law and regulation in democratic constitutions and delegate to the executive [*governo*] a legislative power that should rest exclusively with parliament, Tingsten seeks to examine the situation that arose in a series of countries (France, Switzerland, Belgium, the United States, England, Italy, Austria, and Germany) from the systematic expansion of executive [*governamentali*] powers during World War One, when a state of siege was declared or full powers laws issued in many of the warring states (and even in neutral ones, like Switzerland). The book goes no further than recording a large number of case histories; nevertheless, in the conclusion the author seems to realize that although a temporary and controlled use of full powers is theoretically compatible with democratic constitutions, "a systematic and regular exercise of the institution necessarily leads to the 'liquidation' of democracy" (333). In fact, the gradual erosion of the legislative powers of parliament—which today is often limited to ratifying measures that the executive issues through decrees having the force of law—has since then become a common practice. From this perspective, World War One (and the years following it) appear as a laboratory for testing and honing the functional mechanisms and apparatuses of the state of exception as a paradigm of government. One of the essential characteristics of the state of exception—the provisional abolition of the distinction among legislative, executive, and judicial powers—here shows its tendency to become a lasting practice of government.

Friedrich's book makes much more use than is apparent of Schmitt's theory of dictatorship, which is dismissed in a footnote as "a partisan tract" (Friedrich [1941] 1950, 664). Schmitt's distinction between commissarial dictatorship and sovereign dictatorship reappears here as an opposition between constitutional dictatorship, which seeks to safeguard the constitutional order, and unconstitutional dictatorship, which leads to its overthrow. The impossibility of defining and overcoming the forces that determine the transition from the first to the second form of dictatorship (which is precisely what happened, for example, in Germany) is the fundamental aporia of Friedrich's book, as it is generally of all theories of constitutional dictatorship. All such theories remain prisoner in the vicious circle in which the emergency measures they seek to justify in the name of defending the democratic constitution are the same ones that lead to its ruin:

> [T]here are no ultimate institutional safeguards available for insuring that emergency powers be used for the purpose of preserving the Constitution. Only the people's own determination to see them so used can make sure of that. . . . All in all the quasi-dictatorial provisions of modern constitutional systems, be they martial rule, state of siege, or constitutional emergency powers, fail to conform to any exacting standard of effective limitations upon a temporary concentration of powers. Consequently, all these systems are liable to be transformed into totalitarian schemes if conditions become favorable to it. (584)

In Rossiter's book these aporias explode into open contradictions. Unlike Tingsten and Friedrich, Rossiter explicitly seeks to justify constitutional dictatorship through a broad historical examination. His hypothesis here is that because the democratic regime, with its complex balance of powers, is conceived to function under normal circumstances, "*in time of crisis a democratic, constitutional government must temporarily be altered to whatever degree is necessary to overcome the peril and restore normal conditions.* This alteration invariably involves government of a stronger character; that is, *the government will have more power and the people fewer rights*" (Rossiter 1948, 5). Rossiter is aware that constitutional dictatorship (that is, the state of exception) has, in fact, become a paradigm of government ("a well-established principle of constitutional government" [4]) and that as such it is fraught with dangers; nevertheless, it is precisely the immanent necessity of constitutional dictatorship that he intends to demonstrate. But as he makes this attempt, he entangles himself in irresolvable contradictions. Indeed, Schmitt's model (which he judges to be "trail-blazing, if somewhat occasional," and which he seeks to correct [14]), in which the distinction between commissarial dictatorship and sovereign dictatorship is not one of nature but of degree (with the decisive figure undoubtedly being the latter), is not so easily overcome. Although Rossiter provides no fewer than eleven criteria for distinguishing constitutional dictatorship from unconstitutional dictatorship, none of them is capable either of defining a substantial difference between the two or of ruling out the passage from one to the other. The fact is that the two essential criteria of absolute necessity and temporariness (which all the others come down to in the last analysis) contradict what Rossiter knows perfectly well, that is, that the state of exception has by now become the rule: "In the Atomic Age upon which the world is now entering, the use of constitutional emergency powers may well become the rule and not the exception" (297); or as he says even more clearly at the end of the book, "In describing the emergency powers of the western democracies, this book may have given the impression that such techniques of government as executive dictatorship, the delegation of legislative power, and lawmaking by administrative degree were purely transitory and temporary in nature. Such an impression would be distinctly misleading. . . . The instruments of government depicted here as temporary 'crisis' arrangements have in some countries, and may eventually in all countries, become lasting peacetime institutions" (313). This prediction, which came eight years after Benjamin's first formulation in the eighth thesis on the concept of history, was undoubtedly accurate; but the words that conclude the book sound even more grotesque: "No sacrifice is too great for our democracy, least of all the temporary sacrifice of democracy itself" (314).

1.6   An examination of how the state of exception is situated in the legal traditions of the Western states reveals a division—clear in principle, but hazier in fact—between orders that regulate the state of exception in the text of the constitution or by a law and those that prefer not to regulate the problem explicitly. To the first group belong France (where the modern state of exception was born in the time of the Revolution) and Germany; to the second belong Italy, Switzerland, England, and the United States. Scholarship is also correspondingly divided between writers who favor a constitutional or legislative provision for the state of exception and others (Carl Schmitt foremost among them) who unreservedly criticize the pretense of regulating by law what by definition cannot be put in norms [*normato*]. Though on the level of the formal constitution the distinction is undoubtedly important (insofar as it presupposes, in the latter case, that acts performed by the government outside of or in conflict with the law can theoretically be considered illegal and must therefore be rectified by a special "bill of indemnity"), on the level of the material constitution something like a state of exception exists in all the above-mentioned orders, and the history of the institution, at least since World War One, shows that its development is independent of its constitutional or legislative formalization. Thus, in the Weimar Republic (where Article 48 of the constitution regulated the powers of the president of the Reich whenever the "public security and order" [*die öffentliche Sicherheit und Ordnung*] were threatened), the state of exception performed a surely more decisive function than in Italy, where the institution was not explicitly provided for, or in France, which regulated it by a law and which also frequently had recourse to the *état de siège* and legislation by decree.

1.7   The problem of the state of exception presents clear analogies to that of the right of resistance. It has been much debated, particularly during constituent assemblies, whether the right of resistance should be included in the text of the constitution. The draft of the current Italian Constitution included an article that read, "When the public powers violate the rights and fundamental liberties guaranteed by the Constitution, resistance to oppression is a right and a duty of the citizen." This proposal, which followed a suggestion by Giuseppe Dossetti, one of the most prestigious of the leading Catholic figures, met with sharp opposition. Over the course of the debate the opinion that it was impossible to legally regulate something that, by its nature, was removed from the sphere of positive law prevailed, and the article was not approved. However, in the Constitution of the German Federal Republic there is an article (Article 20) that unequivocally legalizes the right of resistance, stating that "against anyone who attempts to abolish that order [the democratic constitution], all Germans have a right of resistance, if no other remedies are possible."

The opposing arguments here are exactly symmetrical to the ones that divide advocates of legalizing the state of exception in the text of the constitution or a special law and those jurists who believe its normative regulation to be entirely inappropriate. It is certain, in any case, that if resistance were to become a right or even a duty (the omission of which could be punished), not only would the constitution end up positing itself as an absolutely untouchable and all-encompassing value, but the citizens' political choices would also end up being determined by juridical norms [*giuridicamente normate*]. The fact is that in both the right of resistance and the state of exception, what is ultimately at issue is the question of the juridical significance of a sphere of action that is in itself extrajuridical. Two theses are at odds here: One asserts that law must coincide with the norm, and the other holds that the sphere of law exceeds the norm. But in the last analysis, the two positions agree in ruling out the existence of a sphere of human action that is entirely removed from law.

‍‍ℵ A BRIEF HISTORY OF THE STATE OF EXCEPTION. We have already seen how the state of siege had its origin in France during the Revolution. After being established with the Constituent Assembly's decree of July 8, 1791, it acquired its proper physiognomy as *état de siège fictif* or *état de siège politique* with the Directorial law of August 27, 1797, and, finally, with Napoleon's decree of December 24, 1811. The idea of a suspension of the constitution (of the "rule of the constitution") had instead been introduced, as we have also seen, by the Constitution of 22 Frimaire Year 8. Article 14 of the *Charte* of 1814 granted the sovereign the power to "make the regulations and ordinances necessary for the execution of the laws and the security of the State"; because of the vagueness of the formula, Chateaubriand observed "that it is possible that one fine morning the whole *Charte* will be forfeited for the benefit of Article 14." The state of siege was expressly mentioned in the *Acte additionel* to the Constitution of April 22, 1815, which stated that it could only be declared with a law. Since then, moments of constitutional crisis in France over the course of the nineteenth and twentieth centuries have been marked by legislation on the state of siege. After the fall of the July Monarchy, a decree by the Constituent Assembly on June 24, 1848, put Paris in a state of siege and assigned General Cavaignac the task of restoring order in the city. Consequently, an article was included in the new constitution of November 4, 1848, establishing that the occasions, forms, and effects of the state of siege would be firmly set by a law. From this moment on, the dominant principle in the French tradition (though, as we will see, not without exceptions) has been that the power to suspend the laws can belong only to the same power that produces them, that is, parliament (in contrast to the German tradition, which entrusted this power to the head of state). The law of August 9, 1849 (which was partially restricted later by the law of April 3, 1878), consequently established that a political state of siege could be declared by parliament (or, additionally, by the head of state) in the case of imminent danger to external or internal security. Napoleon III had recourse several times to this law and, once installed in power, he transferred, in the constitution of January 1852, the exclusive power to proclaim a state of siege to the head of state. The Franco-Prussian War and the insurrection of the Commune coincided with an unprecedented generalization of the state of exception, which was proclaimed in forty departments and lasted in some of them until 1876. On the basis of these experiences, and after MacMahon's failed coup d'état in May 1877, the law of 1849 was modified to establish that a state of siege could be declared only with a law (or, if the Chamber of Deputies was not in session, by the head of state, who was then obligated to convene parliament within two days) in the event of "imminent danger resulting from foreign war or armed insurrection" (law of April 3, 1878, Art. 1).

World War One coincided with a permanent state of exception in the majority of the warring countries. On August 2, 1914, President Poincaré issued a decree that put the entire country in a state of siege, and this decree was converted into law by parliament two days later. The state of siege remained in force until October 12, 1919. Although the activity of parliament, which was suspended during the first six months of the war, recommenced in January 1915, many of the laws passed were, in truth, pure and simple delegations of legislative power to the executive, such as the law of February 10, 1918, which granted the government an all but absolute power to regulate by decree the production and trade of foodstuffs. As Tingsten has observed, in this way the executive power was transformed into a legislative organ in the material sense of the term (Tingsten

1934, 18). In any case, it was during this period that exceptional legislation by executive [*governativo*] decree (which is now perfectly familiar to us) became a regular practice in the European democracies.

Predictably, the expansion of the executive's powers into the legislative sphere continued after the end of hostilities, and it is significant that military emergency now ceded its place to economic emergency (with an implicit assimilation between war and economics). In January 1924, at a time of serious crisis that threatened the stability of the franc, the Poincaré government asked for full powers over financial matters. After a bitter debate, in which the opposition pointed out that this was tantamount to parliament renouncing its own constitutional powers, the law was passed on March 22, with a four-month limit on the government's special powers. Analogous measures were brought to a vote in 1935 by the Laval government, which issued more than five hundred decrees "having force of law" in order to avoid the devaluation of the franc. The opposition from the left, led by Léon Blum, strongly opposed this "fascist" practice, but it is significant that once the Left took power with the Popular Front, it asked parliament in June 1937 for full powers in order to devalue the franc, establish exchange control, and impose new taxes. As has been observed (Rossiter 1948, 123), this meant that the new practice of legislation by executive [*governativo*] decree, which had been inaugurated during the war, was by now a practice accepted by all political sides. On June 30, 1937, the powers that had been denied Blum were granted to the Chautemps government, in which several key ministries were entrusted to nonsocialists. And on April 10, 1938, Édouard Daladier requested and obtained from parliament exceptional powers to legislate by decree in order to cope with both the threat of Nazi Germany and the economic crisis. It can therefore be said that until the end of the Third Republic "the normal procedures of parliamentary democracy were in a state of suspension" (124). When we study the birth of the so-called dictatorial regimes in Italy and Germany, it is important not to forget this concurrent process that transformed the democratic constitutions between the two world wars. Under the pressure of the paradigm of the state of exception, the entire politico-constitutional life of Western societies began gradually to assume a new form, which has perhaps only today reached its full development. In December 1939, after the outbreak of the war, the Daladier government obtained the power to take by decree all measures necessary to ensure the defense of the nation. Parliament remained in session (except when it was suspended for a month in order to deprive the communist parliamentarians of their immunity), but all legislative activity lay firmly in the hands of the executive. By the time Marshal Pétain assumed power, the French parliament was a shadow of itself. Nevertheless, the Constitutional Act of July 11, 1940, granted the head of state the power to proclaim a state of siege throughout the entire national territory (which by then was partially occupied by the German army).

In the present constitution, the state of exception is regulated by Article 16, which De Gaulle had proposed. The article establishes that the president of the Republic may take all necessary measures "when the institutions of the Republic, the independence of the Nation, the integrity of its territory, or the execution of its international commitments are seriously and immediately threatened and the regular functioning of the constitutional public powers is interrupted." In April 1961, during the Algerian crisis, De Gaulle had recourse to Article 16 even though the functioning of the public powers had not been interrupted. Since that time, Article 16 has never again been invoked, but, in conformity with a continuing tendency in all of the Western democracies, the declaration of the state of exception has gradually been replaced by an unprecedented generalization of the paradigm of security as the normal technique of government.

The history of Article 48 of the Weimar Constitution is so tightly woven into the history of Germany between the wars that it is impossible to understand Hitler's rise to power without first analyzing the uses and abuses of this article in the years between 1919 and 1933. Its immediate precedent was Article 68 of the Bismarckian Constitution, which, in cases where "public security was threatened in the territory of the Reich," granted the emperor the power to declare a part of the Reich to be in a state of war (*Kriegszustand*), whose conditions and limitations followed those set forth in the Prussian law of June 4, 1851, concerning the state of siege. Amid the disorder and rioting that followed the end of the war, the deputies of the National Assembly that was to vote on the new constitution (assisted by jurists among whom the name of Hugo Preuss stands out) included an article that granted the president of the Reich extremely broad emergency [*eccezionali*] powers. The text of Article 48 reads, "If security and public order are seriously [*erheblich*] disturbed or threatened in the German Reich, the president of the Reich may take the measures necessary to reestablish security and public order, with the help of the armed forces if required. To this end he may wholly or partially suspend the fundamental rights [*Grundrechte*] established in Articles 114, 115, 117, 118, 123, 124, and 153." The article added that a law would specify in detail the conditions and limitations under which this presidential power was to be exercised. Since that law was never passed, the president's emergency [*eccezionali*] powers remained so indeterminate that not only did theorists regularly use the phrase "presidential dictatorship" in reference to Article 48, but in 1925 Schmitt could write that "no constitution on earth had so easily legalized a coup d'état as did the Weimar Constitution" (Schmitt 1995, 25).

Save for a relative pause between 1925 and 1929, the governments of the Republic, beginning with Brüning's, made continual use of Article 48, proclaiming a state of exception and issuing emergency decrees on more than two hundred and fifty occasions; among other things, they employed it to imprison thousands of communist militants and to set up special tribunals authorized to pronounce capital sentences. On several occasions, particularly in October 1923, the government had recourse to Article 48 to cope with the fall of the mark, thus confirming the modern tendency to conflate politico-military and economic crises.

It is well known that the last years of the Weimar Republic passed entirely under a regime of the state of exception; it is less obvious to note that Hitler could probably not have taken power had the country not been under a regime of presidential dictatorship for nearly three years and had parliament been functioning. In July 1930, the Brüning government was put in the minority, but Brüning did not resign. Instead, President Hindenburg granted him recourse to Article 48 and dissolved the Reichstag. From that moment on, Germany in fact ceased to be a parliamentary republic. Parliament met only seven times for no longer than twelve months in all, while a fluctuating coalition of Social Democrats and centrists stood by and watched a government that by then answered only to the president of the Reich. In 1932, Hindenburg—reelected president over Hitler and Thälmann—forced Brüning to resign and named the centrist von Papen to his post. On June 4, the Reichstag was dissolved and never reconvened until the advent of Nazism. On July 20, a state of exception was proclaimed in the Prussian territory, and von Papen was named Reich Commissioner for Prussia—ousting Otto Braun's Social Democratic government.

The state of exception in which Germany found itself during the Hindenburg presidency was justified by Schmitt on a constitutional level by the idea that the president acted as the "guardian of the constitution" (Schmitt 1931); but the end of the Weimar Republic clearly demonstrates that, on the contrary, a "protected democracy" is not a democracy at all, and that the paradigm of constitutional dictatorship functions instead as a transitional phase that leads inevitably to the establishment of a totalitarian regime.

Given these precedents, it is understandable that the constitution of the Federal Republic did not mention the state of exception. Nevertheless, on June 24, 1968, the "grand coalition" of Christian Democrats and Social Democrats passed a law for the amendment of the constitution (*Gesetz zur Ergänzung des Grundgesetzes*) that reintroduced the state of exception (defined as the "state of internal necessity," *innere Notstand*). However, with an unintended irony, for the first time in the history of the institution, the proclamation of the state of exception was provided for not simply to safeguard public order and security, but to defend the "liberal-democratic constitution." By this point, protected democracy had become the rule.

On August 3, 1914, the Swiss Federal Assembly granted the Federal Council "the unlimited power to take all measures necessary to guarantee the security, integrity, and neutrality of Switzerland." This unusual act—by virtue of which a non-warring state granted powers to the executive that were even vaster and vaguer than those received by the governments of countries directly involved in the war—is of interest because of the debates it provoked both in the assembly itself and in the Swiss Federal Court when the citizens objected that the act was unconstitutional. The tenacity with which on this occasion the Swiss jurists (nearly thirty years ahead of the theorists of constitutional dictatorship) sought (like Waldkirch and Burckhardt) to derive the legitimacy of the state of exception from the text of the constitution itself (specifically, Article 2, which read, "the aim of the Confederation is to ensure the independence of the fatherland against the foreigner [and] to maintain internal tranquility and order"), or (like Hoerni and Fleiner) to ground the state of exception in a law of necessity "inherent in the very existence of the State," or (like His) in a juridical lacuna that the exceptional provisions must fill, shows that the theory of the state of exception is by no means the exclusive legacy of the antidemocratic tradition.

In Italy the history and legal situation of the state of exception are of particular interest with regard to legislation by emergency executive [*governativi*] decrees (the so-called law-decrees). Indeed, from this viewpoint one could say that Italy functioned as a true and proper juridico-political laboratory for organizing the process (which was also occurring to differing degrees in other European states) by which the law-decree "changed from a derogatory and exceptional instrument for normative production to an ordinary source for the production of law" (Fresa 1981, 156). But this also means that one of the essential paradigms through which democracy is transformed from parliamentary to executive [*governamentale*] was elaborated precisely by a state whose governments were often unstable. In any case, it is in this context that the emergency decree's pertinence to the problematic sphere of the state of exception comes clearly into view. The

Albertine Statute (like the current Republican Constitution) made no mention of the state of exception. Nevertheless, the governments of the kingdom resorted to proclaiming a state of siege many times: in Palermo and the Sicilian provinces in 1862 and 1866, in Naples in 1862, in Sicily and Lunigiana in 1894, and in Naples and Milan in 1898, where the repression of the disturbances was particularly bloody and provoked bitter debates in parliament. The declaration of a state of siege on the occasion of the earthquake of Messina and Reggio Calabria on December 28, 1908 is only apparently a different situation. Not only was the state of siege ultimately proclaimed for reasons of public order—that is, to suppress the robberies and looting provoked by the disaster—but from a theoretical standpoint, it is also significant that these acts furnished the occasion that allowed Santi Romano and other Italian jurists to elaborate the thesis (which we examine in some detail later) that necessity is the primary source of law.

In each of these cases, the state of siege was proclaimed by a royal decree that, while not requiring parliamentary ratification, was nevertheless always approved by parliament, as were other emergency decrees not related to the state of siege (in 1923 and 1924 several thousand outstanding law-decrees issued in the preceding years were thus converted into law). In 1926 the Fascist regime had a law issued that expressly regulated the matter of the law-decrees. Article 3 of this law established that, upon deliberation of the council of ministers, "norms having force of law" could be issued by royal decree "(1) when the government is delegated to do so by a law within the limits of the delegation, and (2) in extraordinary situations, in which it is required for reasons of urgent and absolute necessity. The judgment concerning necessity and urgency is not subject to any oversight other than parliament's political oversight." The decrees provided for in the second clause had to be presented to parliament for conversion into law; but parliament's total loss of autonomy during the Fascist regime rendered this condition superfluous.

Although the Fascist governments' abuse of emergency decrees was so great that in 1939 the regime itself felt it necessary to limit their reach, Article 77 of the Republican Constitution established with singular continuity that "in extraordinary situations of necessity and emergency" the government could adopt "provisional measures having force of law," which had to be presented the same day to parliament and which went out of effect if not converted into law within sixty days of their issuance.

It is well known that since then the practice of executive [*governamentale*] legislation by law-decrees has become the rule in Italy. Not only have emergency

decrees been issued in moments of political crisis, thus circumventing the constitutional principle that the rights of the citizens can be limited only by law
(see, for example, the decrees issued for the repression of terrorism: the law-
decree of March 28, 1978, n. 59, converted into the law of May 21 1978, n. 191
[the so-called Moro Law], and the law-decree of December 15, 1979, n. 625, converted into the law of February 6, 1980, n. 15), but law-decrees now constitute
the normal form of legislation to such a degree that they have been described
as "bills strengthened by guaranteed emergency" (Fresa 1981, 152). This means
that the democratic principle of the separation of powers has today collapsed
and that the executive power has in fact, at least partially, absorbed the legislative power. Parliament is no longer the sovereign legislative body that holds the
exclusive power to bind the citizens by means of the law: it is limited to ratifying the decrees issued by the executive power. In a technical sense, the Italian
Republic is no longer parliamentary, but executive [*governamentale*]. And it is
significant that though this transformation of the constitutional order (which is
today underway to varying degrees in all the Western democracies) is perfectly
well known to jurists and politicians, it has remained entirely unnoticed by the
citizens. At the very moment when it would like to give lessons in democracy
to different traditions and cultures, the political culture of the West does not
realize that it has entirely lost its canon.

The only legal apparatus in England that is comparable to the French *état de
siège* goes by the term *martial law;* but this concept is so vague that it has been
rightly described as an "unlucky name for the justification by the common law
of acts done by necessity for the defence of the Commonwealth when there
is war within the realm" (Rossiter 1948, 142). This, however, does not mean
that something like a state of exception could not exist. In the Mutiny Acts,
the Crown's power to declare martial law was generally confined to times of
war; nevertheless, it necessarily entailed sometimes serious consequences for
the civilians who found themselves factually involved in the armed repression.
Thus Schmitt sought to distinguish martial law from the military tribunals and
summary proceedings that at first applied only to soldiers, in order to conceive
of it as a purely factual proceeding and draw it closer to the state of exception:
"Despite the name it bears, martial law is neither a right nor a law in this sense,
but rather a proceeding guided essentially by the necessity of achieving a certain
end" (Schmitt 1921, 172).

    World War One played a decisive role in the generalization of exceptional executive [*governamentali*] apparatuses in England as well. Indeed, immediately after war was declared, the government asked parliament to approve a series of emergency measures that had been prepared by the relevant ministers, and they were passed virtually without discussion. The most important of these acts was the Defence of the Realm Act of August 4, 1914, known as DORA, which not only granted the government quite vast powers to regulate the wartime economy, but also provided for serious limitations on the fundamental rights of the citizens (in particular, granting military tribunals jurisdiction over civilians). The activity of parliament saw a significant eclipse for the entire duration of the war, just as in France. And in England too this process went beyond the emergency of the war, as is shown by the approval—on October 29, 1920, in a time of strikes and social tensions—of the Emergency Powers Act. Indeed, Article 1 of the act stated that

> [i]f at any time it appears to His Majesty that any action has been taken or is immediately threatened by any persons or body of persons of such a nature and on so extensive a scale as to be calculated, by interfering with the supply and distribution of food, water, fuel, or light, or with the means of locomotion, to deprive the community, or any substantial portion of the community, of the essentials of life, His Majesty may, by proclamation (hereinafter referred to as a proclamation of emergency), declare that a state of emergency exists.

Article 2 of the law gave His Majesty in Council the power to issue regulations and to grant the executive the "powers and duties . . . necessary for the preservation of the peace," and it introduced special courts ("courts of summary jurisdiction") for offenders. Even though the penalties imposed by these courts could not exceed three months in jail ("with or without hard labor"), the principle of the state of exception had been firmly introduced into English law.

The place—both logical and pragmatic—of a theory of the state of exception in the American constitution is in the dialectic between the powers of the president and those of Congress. This dialectic has taken shape historically (and in an exemplary way already beginning with the Civil War) as a conflict over supreme authority in an emergency situation; or, in Schmittian terms (and this is surely significant in a country considered to be the cradle of democracy), as a conflict over sovereign decision.

The textual basis of the conflict lies first of all in Article 1 of the constitution, which establishes that "[t]he Privilege of the Writ of Habeas Corpus shall not be suspended, unless when in Cases of Rebellion or Invasion the public Safety may require it" but does not specify which authority has the jurisdiction to decide on the suspension (even though prevailing opinion and the context of the passage itself lead one to assume that the clause is directed at Congress and not the president). The second point of conflict lies in the relation between another passage of Article 1 (which declares that the power to declare war and to raise and support the army and navy rests with Congress) and Article 2, which states that "[t]he President shall be Commander in Chief of the Army and Navy of the United States."

Both of these problems reach their critical threshold with the Civil War (1861–1865). Acting counter to the text of Article 1, on April 15, 1861, Lincoln decreed that an army of seventy-five thousand men was to be raised and convened a special session of Congress for July 4. In the ten weeks that passed between April 15 and July 4, Lincoln in fact acted as an absolute dictator (for this reason, in his book *Dictatorship,* Schmitt can refer to it as a perfect example of commissarial dictatorship: see 1921, 136). On April 27, with a technically even more significant decision, he authorized the General in Chief of the Army to suspend the writ of habeas corpus whenever he deemed it necessary along military lines between Washington and Philadelphia, where there had been disturbances. Furthermore, the president's autonomy in deciding on extraordinary measures continued even after Congress was convened (thus, on February 14, 1862, Lincoln imposed censorship of the mail and authorized the arrest and detention in military prisons of persons suspected of "disloyal and treasonable practices").

In the speech he delivered to Congress when it was finally convened on July 4, the president openly justified his actions as the holder of a supreme power to violate the constitution in a situation of necessity. "Whether strictly legal or not," he declared, the measures he had adopted had been taken "under what appeared to be a popular demand and a public necessity" in the certainty that Congress would ratify them. They were based on the conviction that even fundamental law could be violated if the very existence of the union and the juridical order were at stake ("Are all the laws *but one* to go unexecuted, and the Government itself go to pieces lest that one be violated?" See Rossiter 1948, 229).

It is obvious that in a wartime situation the conflict between the president and Congress is essentially theoretical. The fact is that although Congress was perfectly aware that the constitutional jurisdictions had been transgressed, it could do nothing but ratify the actions of the president, as it did on August 6, 1861. Strengthened by this approval, on September 22, 1862, the president proclaimed the emancipation of the slaves on his authority alone and, two days later, generalized the state of exception throughout the entire territory of the United States, authorizing the arrest and trial before courts martial of "all Rebels and Insurgents, their aiders and abettors within the United States, and all persons discouraging volunteer enlistments, resisting militia drafts, or guilty of any disloyal practice, affording aid and comfort to Rebels against the authority of the United States." By this point, the president of the United States was the holder of the sovereign decision on the state of exception.

According to American historians, during World War One President Woodrow Wilson personally assumed even broader powers than those Abraham Lincoln had claimed. It is, however, necessary to specify that instead of ignoring Congress, as Lincoln had done, Wilson preferred each time to have the powers in question delegated to him by Congress. In this regard, his practice of government is closer to the one that would prevail in Europe in the same years, or to the current one, which instead of declaring the state of exception prefers to have exceptional laws issued. In any case, from 1917 to 1918, Congress approved a series of acts (from the Espionage Act of June 1917 to the Overman Act of May 1918) that granted the president complete control over the administration of the country and not only prohibited disloyal activities (such as collaboration with the enemy and the diffusion of false reports), but even made it a crime to "willfully utter, print, write, or publish any disloyal, profane, scurrilous, or abusive language about the form of government of the United States."

Because the sovereign power of the president is essentially grounded in the emergency linked to a state of war, over the course of the twentieth century the metaphor of war becomes an integral part of the presidential political vocabulary whenever decisions considered to be of vital importance are being imposed. Thus, in 1933, Franklin D. Roosevelt was able to assume extraordinary powers to cope with the Great Depression by presenting his actions as those of a commander during a military campaign:

I assume unhesitatingly the leadership of this great army of our people dedicated to a disciplined attack upon our common problems. . . . I am prepared under my constitutional duty to recommend the measures that a stricken Nation in the midst of a stricken world may require. . . . But in the event that the Congress shall fail to take [the necessary measures] and in the event that the national emergency is still critical, I shall not evade the clear course of duty that will then confront me. I shall ask the Congress for the one remaining instrument to meet the crisis—broad Executive power to wage war against the emergency, as great as the power that would be given to me if we were in fact invaded by a foreign foe. (Roosevelt 1938, 14–15)

It is well not to forget that, from the constitutional standpoint, the New Deal was realized by delegating to the president (through a series of statutes culminating in the National Recovery Act of June 16, 1933) an unlimited power to regulate and control every aspect of the economic life of the country—a fact that is in perfect conformity with the already mentioned parallelism between military and economic emergencies that characterizes the politics of the twentieth century.

The outbreak of World War Two extended these powers with the proclamation of a "limited" national emergency on September 8, 1939, which became unlimited on May 27, 1941. On September 7, 1942, while requesting that Congress repeal a law concerning economic matters, the president renewed his claim to sovereign powers during the emergency: "In the event that the Congress should fail to act, and act adequately, I shall accept the responsibility, and I will act. . . . The American people can . . . be sure that I shall not hesitate to use every power vested in me to accomplish the defeat of our enemies in any part of the world where our own safety demands such defeat" (Rossiter 1948, 268–69). The most spectacular violation of civil rights (all the more serious because of its solely racial motivation) occurred on February 19, 1942, with the internment of seventy thousand American citizens of Japanese descent who resided on the West Coast (along with forty thousand Japanese citizens who lived and worked there).

President Bush's decision to refer to himself constantly as the "Commander in Chief of the Army" after September 11, 2001, must be considered in the context of this presidential claim to sovereign powers in emergency situations. If, as we have seen, the assumption of this title entails a direct reference to the state of exception, then Bush is attempting to produce a situation in which the emergency becomes the rule, and the very distinction between peace and war (and between foreign and civil war) becomes impossible.

1.8   The differences in the legal traditions correspond in scholarship to the division between those who seek to include the state of exception within the sphere of the juridical order and those who consider it something external, that is, an essentially political, or in any case extrajuridical, phenomenon. Among the former, some (such as Santi Romano, Hauriou, and Mortati) understand the state of exception to be an integral part of positive law because the necessity that grounds it acts as an autonomous source of law, while others (such as Hoerni, Ranelletti, and Rossiter) conceive of it as the state's subjective (natural or constitutional) right to its own preservation. Those in the latter group (such as Biscaretti, Balladore-Pallieri, and Carré de Malberg) instead consider the state of exception and the necessity that grounds it to be essentially extrajuridical, de facto elements, even though they may have consequences in the sphere of law. Julius Hatschek has summarized the various positions in the contrast between an *objektive Notstandstheorie*, according to which every act performed outside of or in conflict with the law in a state of necessity is contrary to law and, as such, is legally chargeable; and a *subjektive Notstandstheorie*, according to which emergency [*eccezionali*] powers are grounded in "a constitutional or preconstitutional (natural) right" of the state (Hatschek 1923, 158ff.), regarding which good faith is enough to guarantee immunity.

The simple topographical opposition (inside/outside) implicit in these theories seems insufficient to account for the phenomenon that it should explain. If the state of exception's characteristic property is a (total or partial) suspension of the juridical order, how can such a suspension still be contained within it? How can an anomie be inscribed within the juridical order? And if the state of exception is instead only a de facto situation, and is as such unrelated or contrary to law, how is it possible for the order to contain a lacuna precisely where the decisive situation is concerned? And what is the meaning of this lacuna?

In truth, the state of exception is neither external nor internal to the juridical order, and the problem of defining it concerns precisely a threshold, or a zone of indifference, where inside and outside do not exclude each other but rather blur with each other. The suspension of the norm does not mean its abolition, and the zone of anomie that it establishes is not (or at least claims not to be) unrelated to the juridical order. Hence the interest of those theories that, like Schmitt's, complicate the topographical opposition into a more complex topological relation, in which the very limit of the juridical order is at issue. In any case, to understand the problem of the state of exception, one must first correctly determine its localization (or illocalization). As we will see, the conflict over the state of exception presents itself essentially as a dispute over its proper *locus.*

1.9   A recurrent opinion posits the concept of necessity as the foundation of the state of exception. According to a tenaciously repeated Latin adage (a history of the *adagia's* strategic function in legal literature has yet to be written), *necessitas legem non habet,* "necessity has no law," which is interpreted in two opposing ways: "necessity does not recognize any law" and "necessity creates its own law" (*nécessité fait loi*). In both cases, the theory of the state of exception is wholly reduced to the theory of the *status necessitatis,* so that a judgment concerning the existence of the latter resolves the question concerning the legitimacy of the former. Therefore, any discussion of the structure and meaning of the state of exception first requires an analysis of the legal concept of necessity.

The principle according to which *necessitas legem non habet* was formulated in Gratian's *Decretum.* It appears there two times: first in the gloss and then in the text. The gloss (which refers to a passage in which Gratian limits himself to stating generically that "many things are done against the rule out of necessity or for whatever other cause" [*pars I. dist. 48*]) appears to attribute to necessity the power to render the illicit licit (*Si propter necessitatem aliquid fit, illud licite fit: quia quod non est licitum in lege, necessitas facit licitum. Item necessitas legem non habet* [If something is done out of necessity, it is done licitly, since what is not licit in law necessity makes licit. Likewise necessity has no law]). But the sense in which this should be taken is made clearer by a later passage in Gratian's text concerning the celebration of the mass (*pars III. dist. 1. c. 11*). After having stated that the sacrifice must be offered on the altar or in a consecrated place, Gratian adds, "It is preferable not to sing or listen to the mass than to celebrate it in places where it should not be celebrated, unless it happens because of a supreme necessity, for necessity has no law" (*nisi pro summa necessitate contingat, quoniam necessitas legem non habet*). More than rendering the illicit licit, necessity acts here to justify a single, specific case of transgression by means of an exception.

This is clear in the way Thomas in the *Summa theologica* develops and comments on this principle precisely in relation to the sovereign's power to grant dispensations from the law (*Prima secundae, q. 96, art. 6: utrum ei qui subditur legi, liceat praeter verba legis agere* [whether one who is subject to law may act against the letter of the law]):

> If observing the letter of the law does not entail an immediate danger that must be dealt with at once, it is not in the power of any man to interpret what is of use or of harm to the city; this can be done only by the sovereign who, in a case of this sort, has the authority to grant dispensations from the law. If there is, however, a sudden danger, regarding which there is no time for recourse to a higher authority, the very necessity carries a dispensation with it, for necessity is not subject to the law [*ipsa necessitas dispensationem habet annexam, quia necessitas non subditur legi*].

Here, the theory of necessity is none other than a theory of the exception (*dispensatio*) by virtue of which a particular case is released from the obligation to observe the law. Necessity is not a source of law, nor does it properly suspend the law; it merely releases a particular case from the literal application of the norm: "He who acts beyond the letter of the law in a case of necessity does not judge by the law itself but judges by the particular case, in which he sees that the letter of the law is not to be observed [*non iudicat de ipsa lege, sed iudicat de casu singulari, in quo videt verba legis observanda non esse*]." The ultimate ground of the exception here is not necessity but the principle according to which "every law is ordained for the common well-being of men, and only for this does it have the force and reason of law [*vim et rationem legis*]; if it fails in this regard, it has no capacity to bind [*virtutem obligandi non habet*]." In the case of necessity, the *vis obligandi* of the law fails, because in this case the goal of *salus hominum* is lacking. What is at issue here is clearly not a *status* or situation of the juridical order as such (the state of exception or necessity); rather, in each instance it is a question of a particular case in which the *vis* and *ratio* of the law find no application.

א We find an example of the law's ceasing to apply *ex dispensatione misercordiae* [out of a dispensation of mercy] in a peculiar passage from Gratian where the canonist states that the Church can elect not to punish a transgression in a situation where the transgressive deed has already occurred (*pro eventu rei* [for the consequence of the thing]: for example in a case where a person who could not accede to the episcopate has in fact already been ordained as bishop). Paradoxically, the law is not applied here precisely because the transgressive act has effectively already been committed and punishing it would anyway entail negative consequences for the Church. In analyzing this text, Anton Schütz has rightly observed that "in conditioning validity by facticity, in seeking contact with an extrajuridical reality, [Gratian] prevents the law from referring only to the law, and thus prevents the closure of the juridical system" (Schütz 1995, 120).

In this sense, the medieval exception represents an opening of the juridical system to an external fact, a sort of *fictio legis* by which, in this case, one acts as if the bishop had been legitimately elected. The modern state of exception is instead an attempt to include the exception itself within the juridical order by creating a zone of indistinction in which fact and law coincide.

א We find an implicit critique of the state of exception in Dante's *De monarchia*. Seeking to prove that Rome gained dominion over the world not through violence but *iure*, Dante states that it is impossible to obtain the end of law (that is, the common good) without law, and that therefore "whoever intends to achieve the end of law, must proceed with law [*quicunque finem iuris intendit cum iure graditur*]" (2.5.22). The idea that a suspension of law may be necessary for the common good is foreign to the medieval world.

1.10   It is only with the moderns that the state of necessity tends to be included within the juridical order and to appear as a true and proper "state" of the law. The principle according to which necessity defines a unique situation in which the law loses its *vis obligandi* (this is the sense of the adage *necessitas legem non habet*) is reversed, becoming the principle according to which necessity constitutes, so to speak, the ultimate ground and very source of the law. This is true not only for those writers who sought in this way to justify the national interests of one state against another (as in the formula *Not kennt kein Gebot* [necessity knows no law], used by the Prussian Chancellor Bethmann-Hollweg and taken up again in Josef Kohler's book of that title [1915]), but also for those jurists, from Jellinek to Duguit, who see necessity as the foundation of the validity of decrees having force of law issued by the executive in the state of exception.

It is interesting to analyze from this perspective the extreme position of Santi Romano, a jurist who had a considerable influence on European legal thought between the wars. For Romano, not only is necessity not unrelated to the juridical order, but it is the first and originary source of law. He begins by distinguishing between, on the one hand, those who see necessity as a juridical fact or even a subjective right of the state, which is ultimately grounded as such in the legislation in force and in the general principles of law, and, on the other hand, those who think necessity is a mere fact and that therefore the emergency [*eccezionali*] powers founded upon it have no basis in the legislative system. According to Romano, both positions, which agree in their identification of the juridical order [*il diritto*] with the law [*la legge*],* are incorrect, insofar as they disavow the existence of a true and proper source of law beyond legislation.

The necessity with which we are concerned here must be conceived of as a state of affairs that, at least as a rule and in a complete and practically effective way, cannot be regulated by previously established norms. But if it has no law, it makes law, as another common expression has it; which means that it itself constitutes a true and proper source of law. . . . It can be said that necessity is the first and originary source of all law, such that by comparison the others are to be considered somehow derivative. . . . And it is to necessity that the origin and legitimation of the legal institution par excellence, namely, the state, and its constitutional order in general, must be traced back, when it is established as a de facto process, for example, on the way to revolution. And what occurs in the initial moment of a particular regime can also repeat itself, though in an exceptional way and with

---

* The two terms here are *diritto* and *legge*, both of which are usually translated in English as "law." While these terms have close correspondences in French (*droit, loi*), Spanish (*derecho, ley*), and German (*Recht, Gesetz*), some of their sense is inevitably lost in the passage to English. Among their meanings, *diritto* carries the sense of law in the abstract, or the entire sphere of law, while *legge* refers to the specific body of rules that a community or state considers binding. Here and in a few other cases where this distinction is critical, I have, following the author's suggestion, rendered *diritto* as "the juridical order" and *legge* as "the law."—Trans.

more attenuated characteristics, even after the regime has formed
and regulated its fundamental institutions. (Romano 1909, 362)

As a figure of necessity, the state of exception therefore appears
(alongside revolution and the de facto establishment of a constitutional
system) as an "illegal" but perfectly "juridical and constitutional" measure that is realized in the production of new norms (or of a new juridical order):

> The formula . . . according to which, in Italian law, the state of siege
> is a measure that is contrary to the law (let us even say illegal) but is
> at the same time in conformity with the unwritten positive law, and
> is for this reason juridical and constitutional, seems to be the most
> accurate and fitting formula. From both the logical and the historical
> points of view, necessity's ability to overrule the law derives from its
> very nature and its originary character. Certainly, the law has by now
> become the highest and most general manifestation of the juridical
> norm, but it is an exaggeration to want to extend its dominion be-
> yond its own field. There are norms that cannot or should not be
> written; there are others that cannot be determined except when the
> circumstances arise for which they must serve. (Romano 1909, 364)

The gesture of Antigone, which opposed the written law to the
agrapta nomima [unwritten laws] is here reversed and asserted in defense of the constituted order. But in 1944, by which time a civil war was
under way in his country, the elderly jurist (who had already studied the
de facto establishment of constitutional orders) returned to consider the
question of necessity, this time in relation to revolution. Although revolution is certainly a state of fact that "cannot be regulated in its course
by those state powers that it tends to subvert and destroy" and in this
sense is by definition "antijuridical, even when it is just" (Romano 1983,
222), it can, however, appear this way only

> with respect to the positive law of the state against which it is di-
> rected, but that does not mean that, from the very different point of
> view from which it defines itself, it is not a movement ordered and
> regulated by its own law. This also means that it is an order that must

be classified in the category of originary juridical orders, in the now well-known sense given to this expression. In this sense, and within the limits of the sphere we have indicated, we can thus speak of a law of revolution. An examination of how the most important revolutions, including the most recent ones, have unfolded would be of great interest for demonstrating the thesis that we have advanced, which could at first sight seem paradoxical: revolution is violence, but it is juridically organized violence. (Romano 1983, 224)

Thus, in the forms of both the state of exception and revolution, the *status necessitatis* appears as an ambiguous and uncertain zone in which de facto proceedings, which are in themselves extra- or antijuridical, pass over into law, and juridical norms blur with mere fact—that is, a threshold where fact and law seem to become undecidable. If it has been effectively said that in the state of exception fact is converted into law ("Emergency is a state of fact; however, as the brocard fittingly says, *e facto oritur ius* [law arises from fact]" [Arangio-Ruiz 1913, 528]), the opposite is also true, that is, that an inverse movement also acts in the state of exception, by which law is suspended and obliterated in fact. The essential point, in any case, is that a threshold of undecidability is produced at which *factum* and *ius* fade into each other.

Hence the aporias that every attempt to define necessity is unable to resolve. If a measure taken out of necessity is already a juridical norm and not simply fact, why must it be ratified and approved by a law, as Santi Romano (along with the majority of writers) believes it must? If it is already law, why does it not last if it is not approved by the legislative bodies? And if instead it is not law, but simply fact, why do the legal effects of its ratification begin not from the moment it is converted into law, but *ex tunc* [from then]? (Duguit rightly notes that this retroactivity is a fiction and that ratification can produce its effects only from the moment at which it occurs [Duguit 1930, 754].)

But the extreme aporia against which the entire theory of the state of necessity ultimately runs aground concerns the very nature of necessity, which writers continue more or less unconsciously to think of as an objective situation. This naive conception—which presupposes a pure factuality that the conception itself has called into question—is easily critiqued by those jurists who show that, far from occurring as an objective given, necessity clearly entails a subjective judgment, and that obviously the only circumstances that are necessary and objective are those that are declared to be so.

> The concept of necessity is an entirely subjective one, relative to the aim that one wants to achieve. It may be said that necessity dictates the issuance of a given norm, because otherwise the existing juridical order is threatened with ruin; but there must be agreement on the point that the existing order must be preserved. A revolutionary uprising may proclaim the necessity of a new norm that annuls the existing institutions that are contrary to the new exigencies; but there must be agreement in the belief that the existing order must be disrupted in observance of new exigencies. In both cases . . . the recourse to necessity entails a moral or political (or, in any case, extrajuridical) evaluation, by which the juridical order is judged and is held to be worthy of preservation or strengthening even at the price of its possible violation. For this reason, the principle of necessity is, in every case, always a revolutionary principle. (Balladore-Pallieri 1970, 168)

The attempt to resolve the state of exception into the state of necessity thus runs up against as many and even more serious aporias of the phenomenon that it should have explained. Not only does necessity ultimately come down to a decision, but that on which it decides is, in truth, something undecidable in fact and law.

‫ Schmitt (who refers several times to Santi Romano in his writings) probably knew of Romano's attempt to ground the state of exception in necessity as the originary source of law. His theory of sovereignty as the decision on the exception grants the *Notstand* a properly fundamental rank, one that is certainly comparable to the rank given it by Romano, who made it the originary figure of the juridical order. Furthermore, he shares with Romano the idea that the juridical order [*il diritto*] is not exhausted in the law [*la legge*] (it is not by chance that he cites Romano precisely in the context of his critique of the liberal *Rechtsstaat*); but while the Italian jurist wholly equates the state with law, and therefore denies all juridical relevance of the concept of constituent power, Schmitt sees the state of exception as precisely the moment in which state and law reveal their irreducible difference (in the state of exception "the state continues to exist, while law recedes" [Schmitt 1922, 13/12]), and thus he can ground the extreme figure of the state of exception—sovereign dictatorship—in the *pouvoir constituant*.

1.11   According to some writers, in the state of necessity "the judge elaborates a positive law of crisis, just as, in normal times, he fills in juridical lacunae" (Mathiot 1956, 424). In this way the problem of the state of exception is put into relation with a particularly interesting problem in legal theory, that of lacunae in the juridical order [*il diritto*]. At least as early as Article 4 of the Napoleonic Code ("The judge who refuses to judge, on the pretence of silence, obscurity or insufficiency of the law, can be prosecuted on the charge of denial of justice"), in the majority of modern legal systems the judge is obligated to pronounce judgment even in the presence of a lacuna in the law [*la legge*]. In analogy with the principle according to which the law [*la legge*] may have lacunae, but the juridical order [*il diritto*] admits none, the state of necessity is thus interpreted as a lacuna in public law, which the executive power is obligated to remedy. In this way, a principle that concerns the judiciary power is extended to the executive power.

But in what does the lacuna in question actually consist? Is there truly something like a lacuna in the strict sense? Here, the lacuna does not concern a deficiency in the text of the legislation that must be completed by the judge; it concerns, rather, a *suspension* of the order that is in force in order to guarantee its existence. Far from being a response to a normative lacuna, the state of exception appears as the opening of a fictitious lacuna in the order for the purpose of safeguarding the existence of the norm and its applicability to the normal situation. The lacuna is not within the law [*la legge*], but concerns its relation to reality, the very possibility of its application. It is as if the juridical order [*il diritto*] contained an essential fracture between the position of the norm and its application, which, in extreme situations, can be filled only by means of the state of exception, that is, by creating a zone in which application is suspended, but the law [*la legge*], as such, remains in force.

2 ℵ Force-of-~~Law~~

2.1   The most rigorous attempt to construct a theory of the state of exception was made by Carl Schmitt, essentially in the books *Dictatorship* and, one year later, *Political Theology*. Because these two books from the beginning of the 1920s describe—with a, so to speak, interested prophesy—a paradigm (a "form of government" [Schmitt 1921, 151]) that has not only remained current but has today reached its full development, it is necessary at this point to present the fundamental theses of Schmitt's theory of the state of exception.

First a few remarks concerning terminology. In the book from 1921 the state of exception is presented through the figure of dictatorship. Dictatorship, however, which encompasses the state of siege, is essentially a "state of exception," and insofar as it presents itself as a "suspension of law," it comes down to the problem of defining a "concrete exception, . . . a problem that up to now has not been held in due consideration by the general theory of law" (Schmitt 1921, xvii). Having thus inscribed the state of exception within the context of dictatorship, Schmitt then distinguishes between "commissarial dictatorship," which has the aim of defending or restoring the existing constitution, and "sovereign dictatorship," in which, as a figure of the exception, dictatorship reaches its, so to speak, critical mass or melting point. The terms *dictatorship* and *state of siege* can thus disappear in *Political Theology*, with the state of exception (*Ausnahmezustand*) taking their place, while the emphasis shifts, at least apparently, from a definition of the exception to a definition of sovereignty. The strategy of Schmitt's theory is therefore a two-stage strategy, whose articulations and aims we will have to understand clearly.

In both books, the *telos* of the theory is the inscription of the state of exception within a juridical context. Schmitt knows perfectly well that because it brings about a "suspension of the entire existing juridical order" (Schmitt 1922, 13/12), the state of exception seems to "subtract itself from any consideration of law" (Schmitt 1921, 137) and that indeed "in its factual substance, that is, in its core, it cannot take a juridical form" (175). Nevertheless, it is essential for Schmitt that in every case some relation to the juridical order be ensured: "Both commissarial dictatorship and sovereign dictatorship entail a relation to a juridical context" (139); "Because the state of exception is always something different from anarchy and chaos, in a juridical sense, an order still exists in it, even if it is not a juridical order" (Schmitt 1922, 13/12).

The specific contribution of Schmitt's theory is precisely to have made such an articulation between state of exception and juridical order possible. It is a paradoxical articulation, for what must be inscribed within the law is something that is essentially exterior to it, that is, nothing less than the suspension of the juridical order itself (hence the aporetical formulation: "In a juridical sense, an order still exists, . . . even if it is not a juridical order").

In *Dictatorship*, the operator of this inscription of an outside of the law within the law is, in the case of commissarial dictatorship, the distinction between norms of law and norms of the realization of law (*Rechtsverwirklichung*) and, in the case of sovereign dictatorship, the distinction between constituent power and constituted power. Indeed, because it "suspends the constitution *in concreto* in order to protect its concrete existence" (Schmitt 1921, 136), commissarial dictatorship ultimately has the function of creating a state of affairs "in which the law can be realized" (137). In commissarial dictatorship, the constitution can be suspended in its application "without thereby ceasing to remain in force, because the suspension signifies solely a concrete exception" (137). On a theoretical level, commissarial dictatorship can thus be wholly subsumed in the distinction between the norm and the techno-practical rules that govern its realization.

The situation is different in sovereign dictatorship, which is not limited to suspending an existing constitution "on the basis of a right that is provided for therein and is therefore itself constitutional" (Schmitt 1921, 137). Rather, it aims at creating a state of affairs in which it becomes possible to impose a new constitution. In this case, the operator that allows the state of exception to be anchored to the juridical order is the distinction between constituent power and constituted power. Constituent power is not, however, "a simple question of force"; it is, rather, "a power that, though it is not constituted in virtue of a constitution, is nevertheless connected to every existing constitution in such a way that it appears as the founding power, . . . and for this reason it cannot be negated even if the existing constitution might negate it" (137). Though it is juridically formless (*formlos*), it represents a "minimum of constitution" (145) inscribed within every politically decisive action and is therefore capable of ensuring the relation between the state of exception and the juridical order even in the case of sovereign dictatorship.

This clarifies why in the preface Schmitt can present the "essential distinction between commissarial dictatorship and sovereign dictatorship" as the "chief outcome of the book," which makes the concept of dictatorship "finally accessible to jurisprudential consideration" (Schmitt 1921, xviii). Indeed, what Schmitt had before his eyes was a "confusion" and "combination" between the two dictatorships that he never tired of denouncing (203). Yet neither the Leninist theory and practice of the dictatorship of the proletariat nor the gradual exacerbation of the use of the state of exception in the Weimar Republic was a figure of the old commissarial dictatorship; they were, rather, something new and more extreme, which threatened to put into question the very consistency of the juridico-political order, and whose relation to the law is exactly what Schmitt sought to preserve at all costs.

In *Political Theology*, on the other hand, the operator of the inscription of the state of exception within the juridical order is the distinction (which had already been proposed in the 1912 book *Gesetz und Urteil*) between two fundamental elements of law: norm (*Norm*) and decision (*Entscheidung, Dezision*). In suspending the norm, the state of exception "reveals [*offenbart*], in absolute purity, a specifically juridical formal element: the decision" (Schmitt 1922, 13/13). The two elements, norm and decision, thus show their autonomy. "Just as in the normal situation the autonomous moment of decision is reduced to a minimum, so in the exceptional situation the norm is annulled [*vernichtet*]. And yet even the exceptional situation remains accessible to juridical knowledge, because both elements, the norm as well as the decision, remain within the framework of the juridical [*im Rahmen des Juristischen*]" (13/12–13).

At this point we can understand why the theory of the state of exception can be presented in *Political Theology* as a theory of sovereignty. The sovereign, who can decide on the state of exception, guarantees its anchorage to the juridical order. But precisely because the decision here concerns the very annulment of the norm, that is, because the state of exception represents the inclusion and capture of a space that is neither outside nor inside (the space that corresponds to the annulled and suspended norm), "the sovereign stands outside [*steht außerhalb*] of the normally valid juridical order, and yet belongs [*gehört*] to it, for it is he who is responsible for deciding whether the constitution can be suspended *in toto*" (10/7).

Being-outside, and yet belonging: this is the topological structure of the state of exception, and only because the sovereign, who decides on the exception, is, in truth, logically defined in his being by the exception, can he too be defined by the oxymoron *ecstasy-belonging*.

ℵ The relationship between *Dictatorship* and *Political Theology* must be seen in the light of this complex strategy of inscribing the state of exception within the law. Jurists and political philosophers have generally directed their attention chiefly to the theory of sovereignty contained in the book from 1922, without realizing that this theory acquires its sense solely on the basis of the theory of the state of exception already elaborated in *Dictatorship*. The rank and the paradox of Schmitt's concept of sovereignty derive, as we have seen, from the state of exception, and not vice versa. And it is certainly not by chance that Schmitt had, in the 1921 book and in previous articles, first laid out the theory and praxis of the state of exception, and only later laid out his theory of sovereignty in *Political Theology*. There is no doubt that his theory of sovereignty represents an attempt to anchor the state of exception unequivocally to the juridical order, but the attempt would not have been possible if the state of exception had not first been articulated within the terms and concepts of dictatorship and, so to speak, "juridicized" through reference to the Roman magistracy and then through the distinction between norms of law and norms of realization.

2.2   Schmitt's theory of the state of exception proceeds by establishing within the body of the law a series of caesurae and divisions whose ends do not quite meet, but which, by means of their articulation and opposition, allow the machine of law to function.

Take on the one hand the opposition between norms of law and norms of the realization of law, between the norm and its concrete application. Commissarial dictatorship shows that the moment of application is autonomous with respect to the norm as such, and that the norm "can be suspended, without thereby ceasing to remain in force" (Schmitt 1921, 137). That is, commissarial dictatorship represents a state of the law in which the law is not applied, but remains in force. Instead, sovereign dictatorship (in which the old constitution no longer exists and the new one is present in the "minimal" form of constituent power) represents a state of the law in which the law is applied, but is not formally in force.

Take now the opposition between norm and decision. Schmitt shows that they are irreducible, in the sense that the decision can never be derived from the content of a norm without a remainder (*restlos*) (Schmitt 1922, 9/6). In the decision on the state of exception, the norm is suspended or even annulled; but what is at issue in this suspension is, once again, the creation of a situation that makes the application of the norm possible ("a situation in which juridical norms can be valid [*gelten*] must be brought about" (13/13). That is, the state of exception separates the norm from its application in order to make its application possible. It introduces a zone of anomie into the law in order to make the effective regulation [*normazione*] of the real possible.

We can, then, define the state of exception in Schmitt's theory as the place where the opposition between the norm and its realization reaches its greatest intensity. It is a field of juridical tensions in which a minimum of formal being-in-force [*vigenza*] coincides with a maximum of real application, and vice versa. But even in this extreme zone—and, indeed, precisely by virtue of it—the two elements of the law show their intimate cohesion.

א The structural analogy between language and law is illuminating here. Just as linguistic elements subsist in *langue* without any real denotation, which they acquire only in actual discourse, so in the state of exception the norm is in force without any reference to reality. But just as concrete linguistic activity becomes intelligible precisely through the presupposition of something like a language, so is the norm able to refer to the normal situation through the suspension of its application in the state of exception.

It can generally be said that not only language and law but all social institutions have been formed through a process of desemanticization and suspension of concrete praxis in its immediate reference to the real. Just as grammar, in producing a speech without denotation, has isolated something like a language from discourse, and law, in suspending the concrete custom and usage of individuals, has been able to isolate something like a norm, so the patient work of civilization proceeds in every domain by separating human praxis from its concrete exercise and thereby creating that excess of signification over denotation that Lévi-Strauss was the first to recognize. In this sense, the floating signifier—this guiding concept in the human sciences of the twentieth century—corresponds to the state of exception, in which the norm is in force without being applied.

2.3   In 1989, at the Cardozo School of Law in New York, Jacques Derrida gave a lecture titled "Force de loi: le 'fondement mystique de l'autorité.' " The lecture, which in truth was a reading of Benjamin's essay "Critique of Violence," gave rise to a wide debate among philosophers as well as jurists, but the fact that that no one attempted to analyze the seemingly enigmatic formula that gave the text its title is an indication not only of the complete separation between philosophical and legal cultures, but also of the latter's decline.

Behind the syntagma *force of law* stands a long tradition in Roman and medieval law, where (at least beginning with Justinian's *Digests, De legibus*, 1.7: *legis virtus haec est: imperare, vetare, permittere, punire* [The capacity of law is this: to command, to forbid, to allow, to punish]) it has the generic sense of efficacy, the capacity to bind. But only in the modern epoch, in the context of the French Revolution, does it begin to indicate the supreme value of those state acts declared by the representative assemblies of the people. Thus, in Article 6 of the constitution of 1791, *force de loi* designates the untouchability of the law, which even the sovereign himself can neither abrogate nor modify. In this regard, modern doctrine distinguishes between the *efficacy* of the law—which rests absolutely with every valid legislative act and consists in the production of legal effects—and the *force of law*, which is instead a relative concept that expresses the position of the law or of acts comparable to it with respect to other acts of the juridical order that are endowed with a force superior to the law (as in the case of the constitution) or inferior to it (such as the decrees and regulations issued by the executive) (Quadri 1979, 10).

The decisive point, however, is that in both modern and ancient doctrine the syntagma *force of law* refers in the technical sense not to the law but to those decrees (which, as we indeed say, have the force of law) that the executive power can be authorized to issue in some situations, particularly in the state of exception. That is to say, the concept of "force of law," as a technical legal term, defines a separation of the norm's *vis obligandi,* or applicability, from its formal essence, whereby decrees, provisions, and measures that are not formally laws nevertheless acquire their "force." Thus, when the Roman sovereign begins to acquire the power to issue acts that tend increasingly to have the value of laws, Roman doctrine says that these acts have the "force of law" (Ulpian, in *Digests,* 1.4.1: *quod principi placuit legis habet vigorem* [because it pleased the sovereign, it has the force of law]; using equivalent expressions, though ones that underscore the formal distinction between the laws and the constitution of the sovereign, Gaius writes *legis vicem obtineat* [let it take the place of law], and Pomponius writes *pro lege servetur* [let it serve for law]).

In our discussion of the state of exception, we have encountered numerous examples of this confusion between acts of the executive power and acts of the legislative power; indeed, as we have seen, such a confusion defines one of the essential characteristics of the state of exception. (The limit case is the Nazi regime, in which, as Eichmann never tired of repeating, "the words of the Führer have the force of law [*Gesetzeskraft*]).") But from a technical standpoint the specific contribution of the state of exception is less the confusion of powers, which has been all too strongly insisted upon, than it is the separation of "force of law" from the law. It defines a "state of the law" in which, on the one hand, the norm is in force [*vige*] but is not applied (it has no "force" [*forza*]) and, on the other, acts that do not have the value [*valore*] of law acquire its "force." That is to say, in extreme situations "force of law" floats as an indeterminate element that can be claimed both by the state authority (which acts as a commissarial dictatorship) and by a revolutionary organization (which acts as a sovereign dictatorship). The state of exception is an anomic space in which what is at stake is a force of law without law (which should therefore be written: force-of-~law~). Such a "force-of-~law~," in which potentiality and act are radically separated, is certainly something like a mystical element, or rather a *fictio* by means of which law seeks to annex anomie itself. But how is it possible to conceive of such a "mystical" element and the way it acts in the state of exception? This is precisely the problem that we must try to clarify.

2.4   The concept of application is certainly one of the most problematic categories of legal (and not only legal) theory. The question was put on a false track by being related to Kant's theory of judgment as a faculty of thinking the particular as contained in the general. The application of a norm would thus be a case of determinant judgment, in which the general (the rule) is given, and the particular case is to be subsumed under it. (In reflective judgment it is instead the particular that is given, and the general rule that must be found.) Even though Kant was perfectly aware of the aporetic nature of the problem and of the difficulty involved in concretely deciding between the two types of judgment (as shown by his theory of the example as an instance of a rule that cannot be enunciated), the mistake here is that the relation between the particular case and the norm appears as a merely logical operation.

Once again, the analogy with language is illuminating: In the relation between the general and the particular (and all the more so in the case of the application of a juridical norm), it is not only a logical subsumption that is at issue, but first and foremost the passage from a generic proposition endowed with a merely virtual reference to a concrete reference to a segment of reality (that is, nothing less than the question of the actual relation between language and world). This passage from *langue* to *parole,* or from the semiotic to the semantic, is not a logical operation at all; rather, it always entails a practical activity, that is, the assumption of *langue* by one or more speaking subjects and the implementation of that complex apparatus that Benveniste defined as the enunciative function, which logicians often tend to undervalue. In the case of the juridical norm, reference to the concrete case entails a "trial" that always involves a plurality of subjects and ultimately culminates in the pronunciation of a sentence, that is, an enunciation whose operative reference to reality is guaranteed by the institutional powers.

In order to pose the problem of application correctly, it must therefore first be moved from the logical sphere to the practical. As Gadamer has shown (1960, 360, 395/378–79, 418), not only is every linguistic interpretation always really an application requiring an effective operation (which the tradition of theological hermeneutics has summarized in the maxim that Johann A. Bengel placed at the beginning of his edition of the New Testament: *te totum applica ad textum, rem totam applica ad te* [apply all of yourself to the text; apply all of it to yourself]), but it is also perfectly obvious (and Schmitt had no difficulty theorizing this obviousness) that, in the case of law, the application of a norm is in no way contained within the norm and cannot be derived from it; otherwise, there would have been no need to create the grand edifice of trial law. Just as between language and world, so between the norm and its application there is no internal nexus that allows one to be derived immediately from the other.

In this sense, the state of exception is the opening of a space in which application and norm reveal their separation and a pure force-of-law realizes (that is, applies by ceasing to apply [*dis-applicando*]) a norm whose application has been suspended. In this way, the impossible task of welding norm and reality together, and thereby constituting the normal sphere, is carried out in the form of the exception, that is to say, by presupposing their nexus. This means that in order to apply a norm it is ultimately necessary to suspend its application, to produce an exception. In every case, the state of exception marks a threshold at which logic and praxis blur with each other and a pure violence without *logos* claims to realize an enunciation without any real reference.

3 א *Iustitium*

3.1   There is an institution of Roman law that can in some ways be considered the archetype of the modern *Ausnahmezustand*, and yet— indeed, perhaps precisely for this reason—does not seem to have been given sufficient attention by legal historians and theorists of public law: the *iustitium*. Because it allows us to observe the state of exception in its paradigmatic form, we will use the *iustitium* here as a miniature model as we attempt to untangle the aporias that the modern theory of the state of exception cannot resolve.

Upon learning of a situation that endangered the Republic, the Senate would issue a *senatus consultum ultimum* [final decree of the Senate] by which it called upon the consuls (or those in Rome who acted in their stead: *interrex* or proconsuls) and, in some cases, the praetor and the tribunes of the people, and even, in extreme cases, all citizens, to take whatever measures they considered necessary for the salvation of the state (*rem publicam defendant, operamque dent ne quid respublica detrimenti capiat* [Let them defend the state, and see to it that no harm come to the state]). At the base of this *senatus consultum* was a decree declaring a *tumultus* (that is, an emergency situation in Rome resulting from a foreign war, insurrection, or civil war), which usually led to the proclamation of a *iustitium* (*iustitium edicere* or *indicere* [to proclaim or declare a *iustitium*]).

The term *iustitium*—which is constructed exactly like *solstitium*— literally means "standstill" or "suspension of the law": *quando ius stat*, as the grammarians explained etymologically, *sicut solstitium dicitur* (*iustitium* means "when the law stands still, just as [the sun does in] the solstice"); or, in the words of Aulus Gellius, *iuris quasi interstitio quaedam et cessatio* (as if it were an interval and a sort of cessation of law). The term implied, then, a suspension not simply of the administration of justice but of the law as such. The meaning of this paradoxical legal institution—which consists solely in the production of a juridical void—is what we must examine here from both a philosophico-political standpoint and from the perspective of the systematics of public law.

א The definition of the concept of *tumultus*, particularly in comparison to war (*bellum*), has led to debates that are not always pertinent. The connection be-, tween the two concepts is already present in ancient sources, for example in the passage from the *Philippics* (8.1) in which Cicero states that "there can be a war without tumult, but no tumult without a war." All evidence suggests that this passage does not mean that tumult is a special or stronger form of war (*qualificirtes, gesteigertes bellum* [see Nissen 1877, 78]); instead, at the very moment of affirming a connection between war and tumult, it places an irreducible difference between them. Indeed, an analysis of the passages from Livy concerning *tumultus* shows that though the cause of a tumult can be (but is not always) an external war, the term technically designates the state of disorder and unrest (*tumultus* is related to *tumor*, which means "swelling, fermentation") that arises in Rome as a result of that event (thus the news of a defeat in the war against the Etruscans gave rise to a tumult and *maiorem quam re terrorem* [greater terror than the thing] [Livy 10.4.2] in Rome). This confusion between cause and effect is clear in the definition found in the Latin dictionaries: *bellum aliquod subitum, quod ob periculi magnitudinem hostiumque vicinitatem magnam urbi trepidationem incutiebat* [any sudden war that brings great alarm to the city on account of the magnitude of the danger and nearness of the enemy] (Forcellini's *Totius Latinitatis Lexicon*). Tumult is not "sudden war," but the *magna trepidatio* that it produces in Rome. This is why, in other cases, the same term can also designate the disorder resulting from an internal insurrection or civil war. The only possible definition capable of comprising all its known uses is the one that sees *tumultus* as "the caesura by means of which, from the point of view of public law, exceptional measures may be taken" (Nissen 1877, 76). The relation between *bellum* and *tumultus* is the same one that exists between war and military state of siege on the one hand and state of exception and political state of siege on the other.

3.2   It can come as no surprise that the reconstruction of something like a theory of the state of exception in the Roman constitution has always put Roman scholars ill at ease, given that, as we have seen, such a theory is generally missing from public law.

In this regard, Mommsen's stance is significant. When, in his *Römi-*

sches Staatsrecht, he has to confront the problem of the *senatus consultum ultimum* and the state of necessity that it presupposes, the best he can do is resort to the image of the right of self-defense [*legittima difesa*] (the German term for self-defense, *Notwehr,* recalls the term for the state of emergency, *Notstand*): "Just as every citizen acquires a right of self-defense in those urgent situations in which the protection of the community fails, so there is also a right of self-defense for the state and for every citizen as such when the community is in danger and the magistratical function breaks down. Though in a certain sense it stands outside of the law [*ausserhalb des Rechts*], it is nevertheless necessary to make the essence and application of this right of self-defense [*Notwehrrecht*] intelligible, at least to the degree to which it lends itself to a theoretical exposition" (Mommsen 1969, 1: 687–88).

Mommsen's affirmation of the state of exception's extrajuridical character and his doubts about the very possibility of presenting it theoretically are matched by certain hesitations and inconsistencies in his discussion that are surprising in a mind such as his, which has been described as rather more systematic than historical. First of all, even though he is perfectly aware of its contiguity with the *senatus consultum ultimum,* he does not examine the *iustitium* in the section dedicated to the state of necessity (Mommsen 1969, 1: 687–97) but in the section that deals with the magistrates' right of veto (263ff.). Furthermore, though he is aware that the *senatus consultum ultimum* refers essentially to civil war (it is the means by which "civil war is proclaimed" [693]), and though he knows that the form of conscription is different in the two cases (695), he does not seem to distinguish between *tumultus* and state of war (*Kriegsrecht*). In the last volume of the *Staatsrecht,* he defines the *senatus consultum ultimum* as a "quasi-dictatorship," introduced into the constitutional system in the time of the Gracchi, and he adds that "in the last century of the Republic, the Senate's prerogative to exercise a law of war over the citizens was never seriously contested" (3: 1243–44). Yet the image of a "quasi-dictatorship" (which will be picked up by Plaumann [1913]) is entirely misleading, for here not only is there no creation of a new magistracy, but indeed every citizen seems to be invested with a floating and anomalous *imperium* that resists definition within the terms of the normal order.

In his description of this state of exception, Mommsen's acumen manifests itself precisely at the point where it shows its limits. He observes that the power in question absolutely exceeds the constitutional rights of the magistrates and cannot be examined from a juridico-formal point of view. He writes,

> If already the mention of the tribunes of the people and the provincial governors, who lack *imperium* or hold it only nominally, prohibits us from considering this appeal [the one contained in the *senatus consultum ultimum*] as merely a call to the magistrates to energetically exercise their constitutional rights, this appears even more clearly on the occasion when, after the *senatus consultum* provoked by Hannibal's offensive, all the ex-dictators, ex-consuls, and ex-censors assumed *imperium* again and retained it until the withdrawal of the enemy. As the call to the censors also shows, this is not a case of an exceptional prorogation of a previously held office, which, moreover, the Senate could not have ordered in this form. Rather, these *senatus consulta* cannot be judged from a juridico-formal standpoint: it is necessity that produces law, and by declaring a state of exception [*Notstand*], the Senate, as the highest advisory authority of the community, adds only the counsel that the now permitted and necessary personal defenses be expediently organized. (1969, 695–96)

Here Mommsen recalls the case of a private citizen, Scipio Nasica, who, when confronted with the consul's refusal to act against Tiberius Gracchus in execution of a *senatus consultum ultimum*, exclaims, "*qui rem publicam salvam esse vult, me sequatur!* [He who wishes that the state be safe, let him follow me!]" and kills Tiberius Gracchus.

> The *imperium* of these commanders in the state of exception [*Notstandsfeldherren*] stands beside that of the consuls more or less as the *imperium* of the praetor or proconsul stands beside consular *imperium*. . . . The power conferred here is the customary one of a commander, and it makes no difference whether it is directed against an enemy who lays siege to Rome or against a citizen who rebels. . . . Moreover, this authority of command [*Commando*], however it may manifest itself, is still less formulated than the analogous power in the

state of necessity [*Notstandscommando*] in a zone *militiae*, and, like it, disappears on its own with the cessation of the danger. (Mommsen 1969, 1: 694–96)

In his description of this *Notstandscommando*, in which any and every citizen seems to be invested with an *imperium* that is floating and "outside of the law," Mommsen came as close as he could to formulating a theory of the state of exception, but he remained on this side of it.

3.3   In 1877, Adolph Nissen, professor at the University of Strasbourg, published the monograph *Das Iusititum. Eine Studie aus der römischen Rechtsgeschichte*. The book, which seeks to analyze a "legal institution that has until now passed nearly unobserved," is interesting for a number of reasons. Nissen is the first to see clearly that the usual understanding of the term as a "court holiday" (*Gerichtsferien*) is entirely insufficient and that, in its technical sense, it must also be distinguished from its later meaning as "public mourning." Let us take an exemplary case of a *iustitium*, the one Cicero describes in *Philippics* 5.12. Confronted with the threat of Marcus Antonius, who is leading an army toward Rome, Cicero addresses the Senate with these words: *tumultum censeo decerni, iustitium indici, saga sumi dico oportere* (I assert that it is necessary to declare a state of *tumultus*, proclaim a *iustitium*, and don the cloaks [*saga sumere* means roughly that the citizens must take off their togas and prepare for combat]). Nissen readily demonstrates that translating *iustitium* here as "court holiday" would simply make no sense; rather, it is a matter of, under exceptional conditions, putting aside the restrictions that the law imposes on the action of the magistrates (in particular, the prohibition that the *Lex Sempronia* established against putting a Roman citizen to death *iniussu populi* [without orders from the people]). *Stillstand des Rechtes*, "standstill and suspension of the law," is the formula that, according to Nissen, both defines the term *iustitium* and translates it to the letter. The *iustitium* "suspends the law and, in this way, all legal prescriptions are put out of operation. No Roman citizen, whether a magistrate or a private citizen, now has legal powers or duties" (Nissen 1877, 105). Nissen has no doubts about the aim of this neutralization of the law: "When the law was no longer able to perform its highest task—to guarantee the public welfare—the law was abandoned in favor of expediency, and just as in situations of necessity the magistrates were released from the restrictions of the law by a *senatus consultum*, so in the most extreme situations the law was set aside. Instead of transgressing it, when it became harmful it was cleared away; it was suspended through a *iustitium*" (98). In other words, according to Nissen, the *iustitium* responds to the same necessity that Machiavelli unequivocally indicated when, in the *Discourses*, he suggested "breaking" the order to save it ("For in a republic where such a provision is lacking, one must either observe the orders and be ruined, or break them and not be ruined" [138]).

Viewing it from the perspective of the state of necessity (*Notfall*), Nissen can thus interpret the *senatus consultum ultimum*, the declaration of *tumultus*, and the *iustitium* as systematically connected. The *consultum* presupposes the *tumultus*, and the *tumultus* is the sole cause of the *iustitium*. These are not categories of criminal law but of constitutional law, and they designate "the caesura by means of which, from the point of view of public law, exceptional measures [*Ausnahmemaßregeln*] may be taken" (Nissen 1877, 76).

א In the syntagma *senatus consultum ultimum*, the term that distinguishes it from other *consulta* is obviously the adjective *ultimus*, which appears not to have received due attention from scholars. That this term has a technical value is demonstrated by the fact that we find it repeated as a definition of both the situation justifying the *consultum* (*senatus consultum ultimae necessitatis*) and the *vox ultima*, the appeal addressed to all citizens for the salvation of the republic (*qui rem publicam salvare vult, me sequatur*).

Ultimus derives from the adverb *uls*, which means "beyond" (as opposed to *cis*, "on this side"). The etymological meaning of *ultimus* is therefore "what is found absolutely beyond, the most extreme." *Ultima necessitas* (*necedo* etymologically means "I cannot go back") indicates a zone beyond which shelter and safety are not possible. The *senatus consultum ultimum* lies at such an extreme outer edge, but if we now ask "With respect to what?" the only possible answer is the juridical order, which indeed gets suspended in the *iustitium*. In this sense, *senatus consultum ultimum* and *iustitium* mark the limit of the Roman constitutional order.

א Middell's monograph (1887), published in Latin (though the modern authors are cited in German), falls far short of a profound theoretical inquiry into the problem. Though, like Nissen, he clearly sees the tight connection between *tumultus* and *iustitium*, Middell emphasizes the formal contrast between *tumultus*, which is decreed by the Senate, and *iustitium*, which must be proclaimed by a magistrate. From this he concludes that Nissen's thesis (the *iustitium* as a total suspension of law) was excessive, for the magistrate could not independently release himself from the restrictions of the laws. Thus rehabilitating the old interpretation of the *iustitium* as a court holiday, Middell lets the meaning of the institution slip away from him. For whoever may have been the person technically qualified to proclaim a *iustitium*, it is certain that it was always and only declared *ex auctoritate patrum* [on the authority of the fathers], and the magistrate (or mere citizen) therefore acted on the basis of a state of danger that authorized the suspension of the law.

3.4   Let us try to pin down the characteristics of the *iustitium* as they emerge from Nissen's monograph and, at the same time, develop his analyses toward a general theory of the state of exception.

First of all, because it brings about a standstill and suspension of the entire juridical order, the *iustitium* cannot be interpreted through the paradigm of dictatorship. In the Roman constitution, the dictator was a specific kind of magistrate whom the consuls had chosen and whose *imperium*, which was extremely broad, was conferred by a *lex curiata* that defined its aims. On the contrary, in the *iustitium* (even in the case where it is a dictator in office who declares it), there is no creation of a new magistracy; the unlimited power enjoyed de facto by the existent magistrates *iusticio indicto* [the *iustitium* having been declared] results not from their being invested with a dictatorial *imperium*, but from the suspension of the laws that restricted their action. Both Mommsen and Plaumann are perfectly aware of this, and for this reason speak not of dictatorship but of "quasi-dictatorship"; however, not only does the "quasi" do nothing to eliminate the ambiguity, it in fact contributes to the institution's being interpreted according to a manifestly erroneous paradigm.

This is equally true for the modern state of exception. The confusion of state of exception and dictatorship is the limitation that prevented both Schmitt in 1921 and Rossiter and Friedrich after World War Two from resolving the aporias of the state of exception. In both cases, the error was self-serving, since it was certainly easier to justify the state of exception juridically by inscribing it in the prestigious tradition of Roman dictatorship than by restoring it to its authentic, but more obscure, genealogical paradigm in Roman law: the *iustitium*. From this perspective, the state of exception is not defined as a fullness of powers, a pleromatic state of law, as in the dictatorial model, but as a kenomatic state, an emptiness and standstill of the law.

‫א‬ In modern public law theory, it is customary to define as dictatorships the totalitarian states born out of the crisis the democracies underwent after World War One. Thus Hitler as well as Mussolini, Franco as well as Stalin, get indifferently presented as dictators. But neither Hitler nor Mussolini can technically be defined as dictators. Mussolini was the head of the government, legally invested with this office by the king, just as Hitler was chancellor of the Reich, named by the legitimate president of the Reich. As is well known, what characterizes both the Fascist and Nazi regimes is that they allowed the existing constitutions (the Albertine Statute and the Weimar Constitution, respectively) to subsist, and— according to a paradigm that has been acutely defined as "dual state"—they placed beside the legal constitution a second structure, often not legally formalized, that could exist alongside the other because of the state of exception. From a juridical standpoint, the term *dictatorship* is entirely unsuitable for describing such regimes, just as, moreover, the clean opposition of democracy and dictatorship is misleading for any analysis of the governmental paradigms dominant today.

‫א‬ Though Schmitt was not a Roman scholar, he nevertheless knew of the *iustitium* as a form of the state of exception ("martial law presupposed a sort of *iustitium*" [Schmitt 1921, 173]), most probably from the monograph by Nissen (who is cited in the book on dictatorship, though in relation to another text). Though he shares Nissen's idea that the state of exception represents "an emptiness of law" (Nissen speaks of a juridical *vacuum*), Schmitt prefers, apropos of the *senatus consultum ultimum*, to speak of a "quasi-dictatorship" (which suggests a knowledge, if not of Plaumann's study from 1913, at least of Mommsen's *Staatsrecht*).

3.5   This anomic space that comes to coincide suddenly with the space of the city is so peculiar that it disorients not only modern scholars but also the ancient sources themselves. Thus in describing the situation created by the *iustitium*, Livy states that the consuls (the highest Roman magistrates) were *in privato abditi*, reduced to the state of private citizens (Livy 1.9.7); on the other hand, Cicero writes apropos of Scipio Nasica's gesture that though a private citizen, in killing Tiberius Gracchus he acted "as if he were a consul" (*privatus ut si consul esset; Tusculan Disputations* 4.23.51). The *iustitium* seems to call into question the very consistency of the public space; yet, conversely, the consistency of the private space is also immediately neutralized to the same degree. In truth, this paradoxical coincidence of private and public, of *ius civile* and *imperium*, and, in the extreme case, of juridical and nonjuridical, betrays the difficulty or impossibility of thinking an essential problem: that of the nature of acts committed during the *iustitium*. What is a human praxis that is wholly delivered over to a juridical void? It is as if when faced with the opening of a wholly anomic space for human action both the ancients and moderns retreated in fright. Though both Mommsen and Nissen unequivocally affirm the *iustitium*'s character as a juridical *tempus mortuum*, for Mommsen there still exists a *Notstandscommando,* which he does not further identify, while for Nissen there remains a *Befehl,* or "unlimited command" (Nissen 1877, 105), which is matched by an equally unlimited obedience. But how can such a command survive in the absence of any legal prescription or determination?

It is from this perspective that one must also view the impossibility (common to both the ancient and modern sources) of clearly defining the legal consequences of those acts committed during the *iustitium* with the aim of saving the *res publica*. The question was of particular importance, for it concerned whether the killing of an uncondemned (*indemnatus*) Roman citizen was punishable or not. Apropos of Opimius's assassination of Caius Gracchus's followers, Cicero already describes as "endless" (*infinita quaestio*) the question of whether or not a person who has killed a Roman citizen while acting in execution of a *senatus consultum ultimum* can be punished (*De oratore* 2.31.134). Nissen, for his part, denies that either the magistrate who had acted in execution of a *senatus consultum* or the citizens who had followed him could be punished once the *iustitium* was over; but he is contradicted by the fact that Opimius was nevertheless brought to trial (though he was acquitted), and Cicero was sentenced to exile as a consequence of his bloody repression of the Catiline conspiracy.

In truth, the entire question is poorly put, for the aporia becomes clear only once we consider that because they are produced in a juridical void, the acts committed during the *iustitium* are radically removed from any juridical determination. From a legal standpoint it is possible to classify human actions as legislative, executive, or transgressive acts. But it is entirely clear that the magistrate or private citizen who acts during the *iustitium* neither executes nor transgresses a law, and even less does he create law. All scholars agree on the fact that the *senatus consultum ultimum* has no positive content; it merely expresses a counsel with an extremely vague formula (*videant consules . . .* [let the consuls see to it . . .]) that leaves the magistrate or whoever acts for him entirely free to act as he sees fit, or even not to act at all. If we wanted at all costs to give a name to a human action performed under conditions of anomie, we might say that he who acts during the *iustitium* neither executes nor transgress the law, but *inexecutes* [*inesegue*] it. His actions, in this sense, are mere facts, the appraisal of which, once the *iustitium* is expired, will depend on the circumstances. But, as long as the *iustitium* lasts, they will be absolutely undecidable, and the definition of their nature—whether executive or transgressive, and, in the extreme case, whether human, bestial, or divine—will lie beyond the sphere of law.

3.6   Let us now try to summarize the results of our genealogical investigation of the *iustitium* in the form of theses.

(1) The state of exception is not a dictatorship (whether constitutional or unconstitutional, commissarial or sovereign) but a space devoid of law, a zone of anomie in which all legal determinations—and above all the very distinction between public and private—are deactivated. Thus, all those theories that seek to annex the state of exception immediately to the law are false; and so too are both the theory of necessity as the originary source of law and the theory that sees the state of exception as the exercise of a state's right to its own defense or as the restoration of an originary pleromatic state of the law ("full powers"). But fallacious too are those theories, like Schmitt's, that seek to inscribe the state of exception indirectly within a juridical context by grounding it in the division between norms of law and norms of the realization of law, between constituent power and constituted power, between norm

and decision. The state of necessity is not a "state of law," but a space without law (even though it is not a state of nature, but presents itself as the anomie that results from the suspension of law).

(2) This space devoid of law seems, for some reason, to be so essential to the juridical order that it must seek in every way to assure itself a relation with it, as if in order to ground itself the juridical order necessarily had to maintain itself in relation with an anomie. On the one hand, the juridical void at issue in the state of exception seems absolutely unthinkable for the law; on the other, this unthinkable thing nevertheless has a decisive strategic relevance for the juridical order and must not be allowed to slip away at any cost.

(3) The crucial problem connected to the suspension of the law is that of the acts committed during the *iustitium*, the nature of which seems to escape all legal definition. Because they are neither transgressive, executive, nor legislative, they seem to be situated in an absolute non-place with respect to the law.

(4) The idea of a force-of-law is a response to this undefinability and this non-place. It is as if the suspension of law freed a force or a mystical element, a sort of legal *mana* (the expression is used by Wagenvoort to describe the Roman *auctoritas* [Wagenvoort 1947, 106]), that both the ruling power and its adversaries, the constituted power as well as the constituent power, seek to appropriate. Force of law that is separate from the law, floating *imperium*, being-in-force [*vigenza*] without application, and, more generally, the idea of a sort of "degree zero" of the law—all these are fictions through which law attempts to encompass its own absence and to appropriate the state of exception, or at least to assure itself a relation with it. Though these categories (just like the concepts of *mana* or *sacer* in the anthropology and religious studies of the nineteenth and twentieth centuries) are really scientific mythologemes, this does not mean that it is impossible or useless to analyze the function they perform in the law's long battle over anomie. Indeed, it is possible that what is at issue in these categories is nothing less than the definition of what Schmitt calls "the political." The essential task of a theory of the state of exception is not simply to clarify whether it has a juridical nature or not, but to define the meaning, place, and modes of its relation to the law.

4 ℵ Gigantomachy Concerning a Void

4.1   It is from this perspective that we will now read the debate between Walter Benjamin and Carl Schmitt on the state of exception. The
exoteric dossier of this debate, which took place in various forms and
at differing levels of intensity between 1925 and 1956, is not very large:
Benjamin's citation of *Political Theology* in *The Origin of German Tragic
Drama;* the *curriculum vitae* of 1928 and Benjamin's letter to Schmitt
from December 1930 (both of which attest to an interest in and admi-
ration for the "fascist public law theorist" [Tiedemann, editorial note,
in Benjamin, *Gesammelte Schriften,* 1.3: 886] and have always appeared
scandalous); and Schmitt's citations of and references to Benjamin in
his book *Hamlet or Hecuba,* written when the Jewish philosopher had
been dead for sixteen years. This dossier was further enlarged with the
publication in 1988 of the letters Schmitt wrote to Hansjörg Viesel in
1973, in which Schmitt states that his 1938 book on Hobbes had been
conceived as a "response to Benjamin [that has] remained unnoticed"
(Viesel 1988, 14; see Bredekamp's observations, 1998, 913).

The esoteric dossier, however, is larger and has yet to be explored in
all its implications. Indeed, we will attempt to demonstrate that the first
document that must be included in the dossier is not Benjamin's reading
of *Political Theology,* but Schmitt's reading of Benjamin's essay "Critique
of Violence" (1921). The essay was published in issue 47 of the *Archiv für
Sozialwissenschaften und Sozialpolitik,* a journal coedited by Emil Led-
erer, who was then a professor at the University of Heidelberg (and later
at the New School for Social Research in New York), and who was one of
the people Benjamin frequented at that time. Now, not only did Schmitt
publish numerous essays and articles (including the first version of *The
Concept of the Political*) in the *Archiv* between 1924 and 1927, but a careful
examination of the footnotes and bibliographies of his writings shows
that from 1915 on Schmitt was a regular reader of the journal (he cites,
among others, the issues immediately preceding and following the one

containing Benjamin's essay). As an avid reader of and contributor to the *Archiv*, Schmitt could not easily have missed a text like "Critique of Violence," which, as we will see, touched upon issues that were essential for him. Benjamin's interest in Schmitt's theory of sovereignty has always been judged as scandalous (Taubes once described the 1930 letter to Schmitt as a "mine that can blow to pieces our conception of the intellectual history of the Weimar period" [Taubes 1987, 27]); turning the scandal around, we will try to read Schmitt's theory as a response to Benjamin's critique of violence.

4.2   The aim of the essay is to ensure the possibility of a violence (the German term *Gewalt* also means simply "power") that lies absolutely "outside" (*außerhalb*) and "beyond" (*jenseits*) the law and that, as such, could shatter the dialectic between lawmaking violence and law-preserving violence (*rechtsetzende und rechtserhaltende Gewalt*). Benjamin calls this other figure of violence "pure" (*reine Gewalt*) or "divine," and, in the human sphere, "revolutionary." What the law can never tolerate—what it feels as a threat with which it is impossible to come to terms—is the existence of a violence outside the law; and this is not because the ends of such a violence are incompatible with law, but because of "its mere existence outside the law" (Benjamin 1921, 183/239). The task of Benjamin's critique is to prove the reality (*Bestand*) of such a violence: "If violence is also assured a reality outside the law, as pure immediate violence, this furnishes proof that revolutionary violence—which is the name for the highest manifestation of pure violence by man—is also possible" (202/252). The proper characteristic of this violence is that it neither makes nor preserves law, but deposes it (*Entsetzung des Rechtes* [202/251–52]) and thus inaugurates a new historical epoch.

Benjamin does not name the state of exception in the essay, though he does use the term *Ernstfall*, which appears in Schmitt as a synonym for *Ausnahmezustand*. But another technical term from Schmitt's vocabulary is present in the text: *Entscheidung*, "decision." Law, Benjamin writes, "acknowledges in the 'decision' determined by place and time a metaphysical category" (Benjamin 1921, 189/243); but this acknowledgment is, in reality, only a counterpart to "the curious and at first discouraging experience of the ultimate undecidability of all legal problems

[*die seltsame und zunächst entmutgende Erfahrung von der letzlichen Un-
entscheidbarkeit aller Rechtsprobleme*]" (196/247).

4.3 The theory of sovereignty that Schmitt develops in his *Political
Theology* can be read as a precise response to Benjamin's essay. While
the strategy of "Critique of Violence" was aimed at ensuring the existence of a pure and anomic violence, Schmitt instead seeks to lead
such a violence back to a juridical context. The state of exception is the
space in which he tries to capture Benjamin's idea of a pure violence
and to inscribe anomie within the very body of the *nomos*. According to
Schmitt, there cannot be a pure violence—that is, a violence absolutely
outside the law—because in the state of exception it is included in the
law through its very exclusion. That is to say, the state of exception is the
device by means of which Schmitt responds to Benjamin's affirmation
of a wholly anomic human action.

The relation between these two texts, however, is even closer than
this. We have seen how in *Political Theology* Schmitt abandons the distinction between constituent and constituted power, which in the 1921
book had grounded sovereign dictatorship, and replaces it with the concept of decision. This substitution acquires its strategic sense only once
it is seen as a countermove in response to Benjamin's critique. For the
distinction between lawmaking violence and law-preserving violence—
which was Benjamin's target—corresponds to the letter to Schmitt's opposition; and it is in order to neutralize this new figure of a pure violence
removed from the dialectic between constituent power and constituted
power that Schmitt develops his theory of sovereignty. The sovereign violence in *Political Theology* responds to the pure violence of Benjamin's
essay with the figure of a power that neither makes nor preserves law, but
suspends it. Similarly, it is in response to Benjamin's idea of an ultimate
undecidability of all legal problems that Schmitt affirms sovereignty as
the place of the extreme decision. That this place is neither external
nor internal to the law—that sovereignty is, in this sense, a *Grenzbegriff*
[limit concept]—is the necessary consequence of Schmitt's attempt to
neutralize pure violence and ensure the relation between anomie and the
juridical context. And just as pure violence, according to Benjamin, can-

not be recognized as such by means of a decision (*Entscheidung* [Benjamin 1921, 203/252]), so too for Schmitt "it is impossible to ascertain with complete clarity when a situation of necessity exists, nor can one spell out, with regard to content, what may take place in such a case when it is truly a matter of an extreme situation of necessity and of how it is to be eliminated" (Schmitt 1922, 9/6–7); yet, with a strategic inversion, this impossibility is precisely what grounds the necessity of sovereign decision.

4.4   If these premises are accepted, then the entire exoteric debate between Benjamin and Schmitt appears in a new light. Benjamin's description of the baroque sovereign in the *Trauerspielbuch* can be read as a response to Schmitt's theory of sovereignty. Sam Weber has acutely observed how Benjamin's description of the sovereign "diverges ever so slightly, but significantly, from its ostensible theoretical source in Schmitt" (Weber 1992, 130). The baroque concept of sovereignty, Benjamin writes, "develops from a discussion of the state of exception, and makes it the most important function of the sovereign to exclude this" (*den auszuschließen* [Benjamin 1928, 245/65]). In substituting "to exclude" for "to decide," Benjamin surreptitiously alters Schmitt's definition in the very gesture with which he claims to evoke it: in deciding on the state of exception, the sovereign must not in some way include it in the juridical order; he must, on the contrary, exclude it, leave it outside of the juridical order.

The meaning of this substantial modification becomes clear only in the pages that follow, where Benjamin elaborates a true and proper theory of "sovereign indecision"; but this is precisely where the interweaving of reading and counterreading becomes tighter. While for Schmitt the decision is the nexus that unites sovereignty and the state of exception, Benjamin ironically divides sovereign power from its exercise and shows that the baroque sovereign is constitutively incapable of deciding.

The antithesis between sovereign power [*Herrschermacht*] and the capacity to exercise it [*Herrschvermögen*] led to a feature peculiar to the *Trauerspiel* which is, however, only apparently a generic feature and which can be illuminated only on the basis of the theory of sovereignty. This is the tyrant's inability to decide [*Entschlußun-fähigkeit*]. The sovereign, who is responsible for making the decision on the state of exception, reveals, at the first opportunity, that it is almost impossible for him to make a decision." (Benjamin 1928, 250/70–71)

The division between sovereign power and the exercise of that power corresponds exactly to that between norms of law and norms of the realization of law, which in *Dictatorship* was the foundation of commissarial dictatorship. In *Political Theology* Schmitt responded to Benjamin's critique of the dialectic between constituent power and constituted power by introducing the concept of decision, and to this countermove Benjamin replies by bringing in Schmitt's distinction between the norm and its realization. The sovereign, who should decide every time on the exception, is precisely the place where the fracture that divides the body of the law becomes impossible to mend: between *Macht* and *Vermögen*, between power and its exercise, a gap opens which no decision is capable of filling.

This is why, with a further shift, the paradigm of the state of exception is no longer the miracle, as in *Political Theology*, but the catastrophe. "In antithesis to the historical idea of restoration, [the baroque] is faced with the idea of catastrophe. And it is in response to this antithesis that the theory of the state of exception is devised" (Benjamin 1928, 246/66)

An unfortunate emendation in the text of the *Gesammelte Schriften* has prevented all the implications of this shift from being assessed. Where Benjamin's text read, *Es gibt eine barocke Eschatologie*, "there is a baroque eschatology," the editors, with a singular disregard for all philological care, have corrected it to read: *Es gibt keine . . .*, "there is no baroque eschatology" (Benjamin 1928, 246/66). And yet the passage that follows is logically and syntactically consistent with the original reading: "and for that very reason [there is] a mechanism that gathers and exalts all earthly creatures before consigning them to the end [*dem Ende*]." The baroque knows an *eskhaton*, an end of time; but, as Benjamin immediately makes clear, this *eskhaton* is empty. It knows neither redemption nor a hereafter and remains immanent to this world: "The hereafter is emptied of everything that contains the slightest breath of this world, and from it the baroque extracts a profusion of things that until then eluded all artistic formulation . . . in order to clear an ultimate heaven and enable it, as a vacuum, one day to destroy the earth with catastrophic violence" (246/66).

It is this "white eschatology"—which does not lead the earth to a redeemed hereafter, but consigns it to an absolutely empty sky—that configures the baroque state of exception as catastrophe. And it is again this white eschatology that shatters the correspondence between sovereignty and transcendence, between the monarch and God, that defined the Schmittian theologico-political. While in Schmitt "the sovereign is identified with God and occupies a position in the state exactly analogous to that attributed in the world to the God of the Cartesian system" (Schmitt 1922, 43/46), in Benjamin the sovereign is "confined to the world of creation; he is the lord of creatures, but he remains a creature" (Benjamin 1928, 264/85).

This drastic redefinition of the sovereign function implies a different situation of the state of exception. It no longer appears as the threshold that guarantees the articulation between an inside and an outside, or between anomie and the juridical context, by virtue of a law that is in force in its suspension: it is, rather, a zone of absolute indeterminacy between anomie and law, in which the sphere of creatures and the juridical order are caught up in a single catastrophe.

4.5   The decisive document in the Benjamin-Schmitt dossier is certainly the eighth thesis on the concept of history, composed by Benjamin a few months before his death. Here we read that "[t]he tradition of the oppressed teaches us that the 'state of exception' in which we live is the rule. We must attain to a concept of history that accords with this fact. Then we will clearly see that it is our task to bring about the real [*wirklich*] state of exception, and this will improve our position in the struggle against fascism" (Benjamin 1942, 697/392).

That the state of exception has become the rule is not a simple intensification of what in the *Trauerspielbuch* appeared as its undecidability. One must not forget here that both Benjamin and Schmitt had before them a state—the Nazi Reich—in which the state of exception proclaimed in 1933 had never been repealed. From the jurist's perspec-

tive, Germany found itself technically in a situation of sovereign dictatorship, which should have led to the definitive abolition of the Weimar
Constitution and the establishment of a new constitution, whose fundamental characteristics Schmitt strove to define in a series of articles
between 1933 and 1936. But what Schmitt could in no way accept was that
the state of exception be wholly confused with the rule. In *Dictatorship*
he had already stated that arriving at a correct concept of dictatorship is
impossible as long as every legal order is seen "only as a latent and inter-
mittent dictatorship" (Schmitt 1921, xiv). To be sure, *Political Theology*
unequivocally acknowledged the primacy of the exception, insofar as
it makes the constitution of the normal sphere possible; but if, in this
sense, the rule "lives only by the exception" (Schmitt 1922, 15/15), what
then happens when exception and rule become undecidable?

From Schmitt's perspective, the functioning of the juridical order ultimately rests on an apparatus—the state of exception—whose purpose
is to make the norm applicable by temporarily suspending its efficacy.
When the exception becomes the rule, the machine can no longer function. In this sense, the undecidability of norm and exception formulated
in the eighth thesis puts Schmitt's theory in check. Sovereign decision is
no longer capable of performing the task that *Political Theology* assigned
it: the rule, which now coincides with what it lives by, devours itself. Yet
this confusion between the exception and the rule was precisely what the
Third Reich had concretely brought about, and the obstinacy with which
Hitler pursued the organization of his "dual state" without promulgat-
ing a new constitution is proof of it. (In this regard Schmitt's attempt to
define the new material relation between the *Führer* and the people in
the Nazi Reich was destined to fail.)

It is from this perspective that Benjamin's distinction in the eighth
thesis between real state of exception and state of exception *tout court*
should be read. The distinction was, as we have seen, already present in
Schmitt's discussion of dictatorship. Schmitt borrowed the term from
Theodor Reinach's book *De l'état de siège*, but while Reinach, referring
to Napoleon's decree of December 24, 1811, opposed an *état de siège
effectif* (or military) to an *état de siège fictif* (or political), Schmitt, in
his tenacious critique of the legal state [*Stato di diritto*], gives the name

"fictitious" to a state of exception that would be regulated by law, with the aim of guaranteeing some degree of individual rights and liberties. Consequently, he forcefully denounces the Weimar jurists' inability to distinguish between the merely factual action of the president of the Reich under Article 48 and a procedure regulated by law.

Benjamin once again reformulates the opposition in order to turn it back against Schmitt. Now that any possibility of a fictitious state of exception—in which exception and normal conditions are temporally and locally distinct—has collapsed, the state of exception "in which we live" is real and absolutely cannot be distinguished from the rule. Every fiction of a nexus between violence and law disappears here: there is nothing but a zone of anomie, in which a violence without any juridical form acts. The attempt of state power to annex anomie through the state of exception is unmasked by Benjamin for what it is: a *fictio iuris* par excellence, which claims to maintain the law in its very suspension as force-of-law. What now takes its place are civil war and revolutionary violence, that is, a human action that has shed [*deposto*] every relation to law.

4.6   The stakes in the debate between Benjamin and Schmitt on the state of exception can now be defined more clearly. The dispute takes place in a zone of anomie that, on the one hand, must be maintained in relation to the law at all costs and, on the other, must be just as implacably released and freed from this relation. That is to say, at issue in the anomic zone is the relation between violence and law—in the last analysis, the status of violence as a cipher for human action. While Schmitt attempts every time to reinscribe violence within a juridical context, Benjamin responds to this gesture by seeking every time to assure it—as pure violence—an existence outside of the law.

For reasons that we must try to clarify, this struggle for anomie seems to be as decisive for Western politics as the *gigantomachia peri tēs ousias,* the "battle of giants concerning being," that defines Western metaphysics. Here, pure violence as the extreme political object, as the "thing" of politics, is the counterpart to pure being, to pure existence as the ultimate metaphysical stakes; the strategy of the exception, which must ensure the relation between anomic violence and law, is the counterpart to the onto-theo-logical strategy aimed at capturing pure being in the meshes of the *logos*.

That is to say, everything happens as if both law and *logos* needed an anomic (or alogical) zone of suspension in order to ground their reference to the world of life. Law seems able to subsist only by capturing anomie, just as language can subsist only by grasping the nonlinguistic. In both cases, the conflict seems to concern an empty space: on the one hand, anomie, juridical *vacuum*, and, on the other, pure being, devoid of any determination or real predicate. For law, this empty space is the state of exception as its constitutive dimension. The relation between norm and reality involves the suspension of the norm, just as in ontology the relation between language and world involves the suspension of denotation in the form of a *langue*. But just as essential for the juridical order is that this zone—wherein lies a human action without relation to the norm—coincides with an extreme and spectral figure of the law, in which law splits into a pure being-in-force [*vigenza*] without application (the form of law) and a pure application without being in force: the force-of-law.

If this is true, then the structure of the state of exception is even more complex than what we have glimpsed of it up to now, and the positions of the two sides that struggle in and for it are even more tightly woven into each other. And just as the victory of one player in a sporting match is not something like an originary state of the game that must be restored, but only the stake of the game (which does not preexist it, but rather results from it), so pure violence (which is the name Benjamin gives to human action that neither makes nor preserves law) is not an originary figure of human action that at a certain point is captured and inscribed within the juridical order (just as there is not, for speaking man, a prelinguistic reality that at a certain point falls into language). It is, rather, only the stake in the conflict over the state of exception, what results from it and, in this way only, is supposed prior to the law.

4.7   It is therefore all the more important to understand correctly the meaning of the expression *reine Gewalt*, "pure violence," as the essential technical term of Benjamin's essay. What does "pure" mean here? In

January 1919 (that is, about a year before drafting the essay) Benjamin, in a letter to Ernst Schoen that takes up and develops motifs already elaborated in an article on Stifter, carefully defines what he means by "purity" (*Reinheit*):

> It is a mistake to postulate anywhere a purity that exists in itself and needs only to be preserved. . . . The purity of a being is *never* unconditional or absolute; it is always subject to a condition. This condition varies according to the being whose purity is at issue; but this condition *never* inheres in the being itself. In other words: the purity of every (finite) being is not dependent on itself. . . . For nature, human language is the condition of its purity that stands outside of it. (Benjamin 1966, 206/138)

This relational rather than substantial conception of purity is so essential for Benjamin that again in the 1931 essay on Kraus he can write that "at the origin of the creature stands not purity [*Reinheit*] but purification [*Reinigung*]" (Benjamin 1931, 365/455). This means that the purity at issue in the 1921 essay is not a substantial characteristic belonging to the violent action in itself; that is to say, the difference between pure violence and mythico-juridical violence does not lie in the violence itself, but in its relation to something external. Benjamin firmly states what this external condition is at the beginning of the essay: "The task of a critique of violence can be summarized as that of expounding its relation to law and justice." Even the criterion of the "purity" of violence will therefore lie in its relation to law (and the topic of justice in the essay is, in fact, discussed only in relation to the ends of law).

Benjamin's thesis is that while mythico-juridical violence is always a means to an end, pure violence is never simply a means—whether legitimate or illegitimate—to an end (whether just or unjust). The critique of violence does not evaluate violence in relation to the ends that it pursues as a means, but seeks its criterion "in a distinction within the sphere of means themselves, without regard for the ends they serve" (Benjamin 1921, 179/236).

Here appears the topic—which flashes up in the text only for an instant, but is nevertheless sufficient to illuminate the entire piece—of

violence as "pure medium," that is, as the figure of a paradoxical "mediality without ends"—a means that, though remaining such, is considered independently of the ends that it pursues. The problem, then, is not
that of identifying just ends but that of "individuating a different kind of
violence that certainly could not be either the legitimate or illegitimate
means to those ends but is not related to them as means at all but in
some different way [*nicht als Mittel zu ihnen, vielmehr irgendwie anders,
sich verhalten würde*]" (Benjamin 1921, 196/247).

What can this other type of relation to an end be? It will be useful
to apply the considerations that we have just developed concerning the
meaning of Benjamin's term "pure" to the concept of "pure" medium
as well. The medium does not owe its purity to any specific intrinsic
property that differentiates it from juridical means, but to its relation
to them. In the essay on language, pure language is that which is not an
instrument for the purpose of communication, but communicates itself
immediately, that is, a pure and simple communicability; likewise, pure
violence is that which does not stand in a relation of means toward an
end, but holds itself in relation to its own mediality. And just as pure
language is not another language, just as it does not have a place other
than that of the natural communicative languages, but reveals itself in
these by exposing them as such, so pure violence is attested to only as
the exposure and deposition of the relation between violence and law.
Benjamin suggests as much immediately thereafter, evoking the image
of violence that, in anger, is never a means but only a manifestation
(*Manifestation*). While violence that is a means for making law never deposes its own relation with law and thus instates law as power (*Macht*),
which remains "necessarily and intimately bound to it" (Benjamin 1921,
198/248), pure violence exposes and severs the nexus between law and
violence and can thus appear in the end not as violence that governs or
executes (*die schaltende*) but as violence that purely acts and manifests
(*die waltende*). And if the connection between pure violence and juridical violence, between state of exception and revolutionary violence,
is thus made so tight that the two players facing each other across the
chessboard of history seem always to be moving a single pawn—force-
of-law or pure means—what is nevertheless decisive is that in each case

the criterion of their distinction lies in the dissolution of the relation
between violence and law.

4.8   It is from this perspective that we must read Benjamin's statement
in the letter to Scholem on August 11, 1934, that "the Scripture without
its key is not Scripture, but life" (Benjamin 1966, 618/453), as well the
one found in the essay on Kafka, according to which "[t]he law which
is studied but no longer practiced is the gate to justice" (Benjamin 1934,
437/815). The Scripture (the Torah) without its key is the cipher of the
law in the state of exception, which is in force but is not applied or is
applied without being in force (and which Scholem, not at all suspecting
that he shares this thesis with Schmitt, believes is still law). According to
Benjamin, this law—or, rather, this force-of-law—is no longer law but
life, "life as it is lived," in Kafka's novel, "in the village at the foot of the
hill on which the castle is built" (Benjamin 1966, 618/453). Kafka's most
proper gesture consists not (as Scholem believes) in having maintained
a law that no longer has any meaning, but in having shown that it ceases
to be law and blurs at all points with life.

In the Kafka essay, the enigmatic image of a law that is studied but no
longer practiced corresponds, as a sort of remnant, to the unmasking of
mythico-juridical violence effected by pure violence. There is, therefore,
still a possible figure of law after its nexus with violence and power has
been deposed, but it is a law that no longer has force or application, like
the one in which the "new attorney," leafing through "our old books,"
buries himself in study, or like the one that Foucault may have had in
mind when he spoke of a "new law" that has been freed from all disci-
pline and all relation to sovereignty.

What can be the meaning of a law that survives its deposition in such
a way? The difficulty Benjamin faces here corresponds to a problem that
can be formulated (and it was effectively formulated for the first time in
primitive Christianity and then later in the Marxian tradition) in these
terms: What becomes of the law after its messianic fulfillment? (This
is the controversy that opposes Paul to the Jews of his time.) And what
becomes of the law in a society without classes? (This is precisely the debate between Vyshinsky and Pashukanis.) These are the questions that

Benjamin seeks to answer with his reading of the "new attorney." Obviously, it is not a question here of a transitional phase that never achieves its end, nor of a process of infinite deconstruction that, in maintaining the law in a spectral life, can no longer get to the bottom of it. The decisive point here is that the law—no longer practiced, but studied— is not justice, but only the gate that leads to it. What opens a passage toward justice is not the erasure of law, but its deactivation and inactivity [*inoperosità*]—that is, another use of the law. This is precisely what the force-of-law (which keeps the law working [*in opera*] beyond its formal suspension) seeks to prevent. Kafka's characters—and this is why they interest us—have to do with this spectral figure of the law in the state of exception; they seek, each one following his or her own strategy, to "study" and deactivate it, to "play" with it.

One day humanity will play with law just as children play with disused objects, not in order to restore them to their canonical use but to free them from it for good. What is found after the law is not a more proper and original use value that precedes the law, but a new use that is born only after it. And use, which has been contaminated by law, must also be freed from its own value. This liberation is the task of study, or of play. And this studious play is the passage that allows us to arrive at that justice that one of Benjamin's posthumous fragments defines as a state of the world in which the world appears as a good that absolutely cannot be appropriated or made juridical (Benjamin 1992, 41).

5 א Feast, Mourning, Anomie

5.1   Roman scholars and legal historians have not yet been able to find a satisfactory explanation for the peculiar semantic evolution that led the term *iustitium*—the technical designation for the state of exception—to acquire the meaning of public mourning for the death of the sovereign or his close relative. Indeed, with the end of the Republic, *iustitium* ceased to mean the suspension of law in order to cope with a tumult and the new meaning replaced the old one so perfectly that even the memory of this austere institution seems to have entirely vanished. At the end of the fourth century CE, the grammarian Charisius could therefore identify the *iustitium* purely and simply with *luctus publicus*. And it is significant that after the debate raised by Nissen's and Middell's monographs, modern scholars have disregarded the question of the *iustitium* as the state of exception and have concentrated solely on the *iustitium* as public mourning. (Ironically evoking the term's old meaning in his study of Germanicus's funeral, William Seston wrote, "the debate was rather lively, but soon nobody thought about it any more" [Seston 1962, 155].) But how did this term that was used in public law to designate the suspension of law in situations of the most extreme political necessity come to assume the more anodyne meaning of a funeral ceremony for a death in the family?

In an extensive study published in 1980, H. S. Versnel attempted to answer this question by proposing an analogy between the phenomenology of mourning—as attested to in the most diverse places by anthropological research—and periods of political crisis, in which social institutions and rules seems suddenly to dissolve. Just as, during periods of anomie and crisis, normal social structures can collapse and social functions and roles break down to the point where culturally conditioned behaviors and customs are completely overturned, so are periods of mourning usually characterized by a suspension and alteration of all social relations. "Whoever characterizes the critical periods as . . . a temporary substitution of order by disorder, of culture by nature, of *kos-mos* by *chaos*, of *nomos* by *physis*, of *eunomia* by *anomia*, has implicitly characterized the period of mourning and its manifestations" (Versnel 1980, 584–85). According to Versnel, who here cites the analyses of the American sociologists Berger and Luckman, "All societies are constructions in the face of chaos. The constant possibility of anomic terror is actualized whenever the legitimations that obscure the precariousness are threatened or collapse" (585).

Here, not only is the *iustitium*'s evolution from the state of exception to public mourning explained by the resemblance between the manifestations of mourning and those of anomie (which simply begs the question), but the ultimate reason for this resemblance is then sought in the idea of an "anomic terror" said to characterize human societies as a whole. Such a concept (which is as inadequate to account for the specificity of the phenomenon as Marburg theology's *tremendum* and *numinosum* were to orient a correct understanding of the divine) refers, in the last analysis, to the darkest spheres of psychology:

> The total effects of mourning (especially for a chief or king) and the complete phenomenology of cyclical transitional-feasts . . . conform completely to the definition of anomy. . . . [E]verywhere there is a (temporary) reversal of the human to the non-human, the cultural to the natural (viewed as its negative contrast), of *kosmos* to *chaos* and of eunomy to anomy. . . . The feelings of grief and disorientation and their individual and collective expressions are not restricted to one culture or to one type of cultural pattern. Apparently they are intrinsic features of humanity and the human condition, which manifest themselves above all in marginal or liminal situations. I would, therefore, gladly agree with V. W. Turner, who, speaking of "unnatural—or rather, anti-cultural or anti-structural—events" in liminal situations, suggests that "perhaps Freud and Jung, in their different ways, have much to contribute to the understanding of these nonlogical, nonrational (but not irrational) aspects of liminal situations." (Versnel 1980, 604–5)

א In this neutralization of the juridical specificity of the *iustitium* by means of an uncritical psychologistic reduction, Versnel had been preceded by Durkheim, who in his monograph entitled *Suicide* (1897) had introduced the concept of anomie into the human sciences. In setting out the category of "anomic suicide" alongside the other forms of suicide, Durkheim had established a correlation between the diminution of society's regulative influence on individuals and a rise in the suicide rate. This was tantamount to postulating (as he does without providing any explanation) a need of human beings to be regulated in their activities and passions: "What is characteristic of man is to be subject to a restraint that is not physical but moral; that is, social. . . . But when a society is disturbed by some painful crisis or by beneficent but abrupt transitions, it is momentarily incapable of exercising this influence; thence come the sudden rises in the curve of suicides which we have pointed out. . . . Anomie, therefore, is a regular and specific factor in suicide in our modern societies" (Durkheim 1897, 279–88/252–58).

Thus, not only is the correspondence between anomie and anxiety taken for granted (while, as we will see, ethnological and folkloristic research show the contrary), but the possibility that anomie has a more intimate and complex relation to law and the social order is also ruled out in advance.

5.2   Equally inadequate are the conclusions of the study published by Seston a few years later. The author seems to be aware of the possible political significance of the *iustitium* as public mourning, insofar as he stages and dramatizes the funeral of the sovereign as a state of exception: "In imperial funerals there survives the memory of a mobilization. . . . Framing the funerary rites within a sort of general mobilization, with all civil affairs stopped and normal political life suspended, the proclamation of the *iustitium* tended to transform the death of a man into a national catastrophe, a drama in which each person was involved, willingly or not" (Seston 1962, 171–72). This intuition, however, comes to nothing, and the nexus between the two forms of *iustitium* is accounted for by once again presupposing that which was to be explained, that is, an element of mourning implicit in the *iustitium* from the start (172–73).

It is Augusto Fraschetti's achievement to have underscored, in his monograph on Augustus, the political significance of public mourning, showing that the link between the two aspects of the *iustitium* lies not in a presumed character of mourning in extreme situations or anomie but in the tumult that the sovereign's funeral can cause. Fraschetti recovers its origins in the violent riots that had accompanied the funerals of Caesar, which were significantly described as "seditious funerals" (Fraschetti 1990, 57). Just as the *iustitium* was the natural response to tumult in the Republican era, "it is clear how the *iustitium* comes to be identified with public mourning through a similar strategy, by which the deaths in the *domus Augusta* are likened to civic catastrophes. . . . The upshot of this is that the *bona* and the *mala* of a single family come to be the concern of the *res publica*" (57). Fraschetti readily shows how, in conformity with this strategy, Augustus, beginning with the death of his nephew Marcellus, would proclaim a *iustitium* every time the family mausoleum was opened.

It is certainly possible to see the *iustitium* (in the sense of public morning) as nothing other than the sovereign's attempt to appropriate the state of exception by transforming it into a family affair. But the connection is even more intimate and complex.

Take, for example, Suetonius's famous description of Augustus's death at Nola on August 19 of the year 14 CE. The old sovereign, surrounded by friends and courtiers, has a mirror brought to him and, after having his hair combed and his sagging cheeks made up, seems solely concerned to know whether he has acted the *mimus vitae*, the "farce of his life," well. And yet, alongside this insistent theatrical metaphor, he stubbornly and almost insolently continues to ask (*identidem exquirens*)—with what is not simply a political metaphor—*an iam de se tumultus foris fuisset*, "if there was now a tumult outside that concerned him." The correspondence between anomie and mourning becomes comprehensible only in the light of the correspondence between the death of the sovereign and the state of exception. The original nexus between *tumultus* and *iustitium* is still present, but the tumult now coincides with the death of the sovereign, while the suspension of the law is integrated into the funeral ceremony. It is as if the sovereign, who had absorbed into his "august" person all exceptional powers (from the *tribunicia potestas perpetua* [perpetual tribunicial power] to the *imperium proconsolare maius et infinitum* [greater and endless proconsular *imperium*]) and who had, so to speak, become a living *iustitium*, showed his intimate anomic character at the moment of his death and saw tumult and anomie set free outside of him in the city. As Nissen had intuited in a limpid formula (which is perhaps the source of Benjamin's thesis according to which the state of exception has become the rule), "exceptional measures disappeared because they had become the rule" (Nissen 1877, 140). The constitutional novelty of the principate can thus be seen as an incorporation of the state of exception and anomie directly into the person of the sovereign, who begins to free himself from all subordination to the law and asserts himself as *legibus solutus* [unbound by the laws].

5.3   The intimately anomic nature of this new figure of supreme power appears clearly in the theory of the sovereign as "living law" (*nomos empsukhos*), which is elaborated among the neo-Pythagoreans in the same years that see the rise of the principate. The formula *basileus nomos empsukhos* is found in Diotogenes's treatise on sovereignty, which was partially preserved by Stobaeus and whose relevance to the origin of the modern theory of sovereignty must not be underestimated. The usual philological myopia has prevented the modern editor of the treatise from seeing the obvious logical connection between this formula and the anomic character of the sovereign, even though this connection is unequivocally stated in the text. The passage in question—corrupt in part, yet nevertheless perfectly consistent—is divided into three points: (1) "The king is the most just [*dikaiotatos*] and the most just is the most legal [*nomimōtatos*]." (2) "Without justice no one can be king, but justice is without law [*aneu nomou dikaiosunē*; Delatte's proposed insertion of the negative before *dikaiosunē* is totally unjustified philologically]." (3) "The just is legitimate, and the king, having become the cause of the just, is a living law" (L. Delatte 1942, 37).

That the sovereign is a living law can only mean that he is not bound by it, that in him the life of the law coincides with a total anomie. Diotogenes explains this a little later with unequivocal clarity: "Because the king has an irresponsible power [*arkhan anupeuthunon*] and is himself a living law, he is like a god among men" (L. Delatte 1942, 39). And yet, precisely because he is identified with the law, he is held in relation to it and is indeed posited as the anomic foundation of the juridical order. The identification between sovereign and law represents, that is, the first attempt to assert the anomie of the sovereign and, at the same time, his essential link to the juridical order. The *nomos empsukhos* is the original form of the nexus that the state of exception establishes between an outside and an inside of the law, and in this sense it constitutes the archetype of the modern theory of sovereignty.

The correspondence between *iustitium* and mourning shows its true meaning here. If the sovereign is a living *nomos*, and if, for this reason, anomie and *nomos* perfectly coincide in his person, then anarchy (which threatens to loose itself in the city upon the sovereign's death, which is to say, when the nexus that joins it to the law is severed) must be ritualized and controlled, transforming the state of exception into public mourning and mourning into *iustitium*. Corresponding to the undecidability of *nomos* and anomie in the living body of the sovereign is the undecidability between state of exception and public mourning in the city. Before assuming its modern form as a decision on the emergency, the relation between sovereignty and state of exception appears in the form of an identity between the sovereign and anomie. Because he is a living law, the sovereign is intimately *anomos*. Here too the state of exception is the—secret and truer—life of the law.

א The thesis that "the sovereign is a living law" found its first formulation in the treatise by Pseudo-Archytas *On Law and Justice*, which was preserved for us by Stobaeus along with Diotogenes's treatise on sovereignty. Whether or not Gruppe's hypothesis that these treatises were composed by an Alexandrine Jew in the first century of our era is correct, it is certain that we are dealing with a group of texts that, under the cover of Platonic and Pythagorean categories, seek to lay the foundations for a conception of sovereignty that is entirely unbound by laws and yet is itself the a source of legitimacy. In Pseudo-Archytas's text this is expressed in the distinction between the sovereign (*basileus*), who is the law, and the magistrate (*arkhōn*), who must only observe the law. The identification between the law and the sovereign leads to the division of the law into a hierarchically superior "living" law (*nomos empsukhos*) and a written law (*gramma*) that is subordinate to it:

> I say that every community is composed of an *arkhōn* (the magistrate who commands), one who is commanded, and, thirdly, the laws. Of these last, the living one is the sovereign (*ho men empsukhos ho basileus*) and the inanimate one is the letter (*gramma*). The law being the first element, the king is legal, the magistrate is in conformity (with the law), the one who is commanded is free and the entire city is happy; but if there is any deviation, then the

sovereign is a tyrant, the magistrate is not in conformity with the law and the community is unhappy. (A. Delatte 1922, 84)

By means of a complex strategy, which is not without analogies to Paul's critique of the Jewish *nomos* (this proximity is also at times textual: Romans 3:21: *khōris nomou dikaiosunē;* Diotogenes: *aneu nomou dikaiosunē;* and in Pseudo-Archytas the law is defined as a "letter," *gramma,* exactly as in Paul), anomic elements are introduced into the *polis* through the person of the sovereign, with evidently no effect on the primacy of the *nomos* (the sovereign is, indeed, "living law").

5.4   The secret solidarity between anomie and law comes to light in another phenomenon, which represents a symmetrical and in some ways inverse figure to the imperial *iustitium.* Folklorists and anthropologists have long been familiar with those periodic feasts (such as the Anthesteria and Saturnalia of the classical world and the charivari and Carnival of the medieval and modern world) that are characterized by unbridled license and the suspension and overturning of normal legal and social hierarchies. During these feasts (which are found with similar characteristics in various epochs and cultures), men dress up and behave like animals, masters serve their slaves, males and females exchange roles, and criminal behavior is considered licit or, in any case, not punishable. That is, they inaugurate a period of anomie that breaks and temporarily subverts the social order. Scholars have always had difficulty explaining these sudden anomic explosions within well-ordered societies and, above all, why they would be tolerated by both the religious and civil authorities.

Contrary to those interpretations that traced the anomic feasts back to agrarian cycles tied to the solar calendar (Mannhardt, Frazer) or to a periodic function of purification (Westermarck), Karl Meuli, with a brilliant intuition, instead related them to the state of suspended law that characterized some archaic juridical institutions, such as the Germanic *Friedlosigkeit* or the persecution of the *wargus* in ancient English law. In a series of exemplary studies, he showed how the disturbances and violent acts meticulously listed in medieval descriptions of the charivari and other anomic phenomena precisely replicate the different phases of the cruel ritual in which the *Friedlos* and the bandit were expelled from the community, their houses unroofed and destroyed, and their wells poisoned or made brackish. The harlequinades described in the unprecedented *chalivali* of the *Roman de Fauvel* (*Li un montret son cul au vent,* / *Li autre rompet un auvent,* / *L'un cassoit fenestres et huis,* / *L'autre getoit le sel ou puis,* / *L'un getoit le bren aus visages;* / *Trop estoient lès et sauvages* [One showed his ass to the wind, / Another smashed a roof, / One broke windows and doors, / Another threw salt in the wells, / And another threw filth in faces; / They were truly horrible and savage]) cease to appear as parts of an innocent pandemonium, and one after the other find their counterpart and their proper context in the *Lex Baiuvariorum* or in the penal statutes of the medieval cities. The same can be said for the acts of harassment committed during masked feasts and children's begging rituals in which children punished whoever denied their obligation to give a gift with acts of violence that Halloween only distantly recalls.

> Charivari is one of the many names (which vary from country to country and region to region) for an ancient and widely diffused act of popular justice, which occurred everywhere in similar, if not identical forms. Such forms are also used as ritual punishments in the cyclical masked feasts and their extreme offshoots, the traditional children's begging rituals; one may therefore immediately draw upon these for an interpretation of charivari-like phenomena. A closer analysis shows that what at first sight seemed simply to be rough and wild acts of harassment are in truth well-defined traditional customs and legal forms, by means of which, from time immemorial, the ban and proscription were carried out. (Meuli 1975, 473)

If Meuli's hypothesis is correct, the "legal anarchy" of the anomic feasts does not refer back to ancient agrarian rites, which in themselves explain nothing; rather, it brings to light in a parodic form the anomie within the law, the state of emergency as the anomic drive contained in the very heart of the *nomos.*

That is to say, the anomic feasts point toward a zone in which life's maximum subjection to the law is reversed into freedom and license, and the most unbridled anomie shows its parodic connection with the *nomos.* In other words, they point toward the real state of exception as the threshold of indifference between anomie and law. In showing the mournful character of every feast and the festive character of all mourning, law and anomie show their distance and, at the same time, their secret solidarity. It is as if the universe of law—and more generally, the sphere of human action insofar as it has to do with law—ultimately appeared as a field of forces traversed by two conjoined and opposite tensions: one that goes from norm to anomie, and another that leads from anomie to the law and the rule. Hence a double paradigm, which marks the field of law with an essential ambiguity: on the one hand, a normative tendency in the strict sense, which aims at crystallizing itself in a rigid system of norms whose connection to life is, however, problematic if not impossible (the perfect state of law, in which everything is regulated by norms); and, on the other hand, an anomic tendency that leads to the state of exception or the idea of the sovereign as living law, in which a force-of-law that is without norm acts as the pure inclusion of life.

The anomic feasts dramatize this irreducible ambiguity of juridical systems and, at the same time, show that what is at stake in the dialectic between these two forces is the very relation between law and life. They celebrate and parodically replicate the anomie through which the law applies itself to chaos and to life only on the condition of making itself, in the state of exception, life and living chaos. And perhaps the moment has come to try to better understand the constitutive fiction that—in binding together norm and anomie, law and state of exception—also ensures the relation between law and life.

6 ℵ *Auctoritas* and *Potestas*

6.1   In our analysis of the state of exception in Rome, we neglected to ask what was the foundation of the Senate's power to suspend the law by means of the *senatus consultum ultimum* and the consequent proclamation of a *iustitium*. Whoever may have been the subject qualified to declare a *iustitium*, it is certain that it was always declared *ex auctoritate patrum*. Indeed, it is well known that in Rome the term designating the Senate's most proper prerogative was neither *imperium* nor *potestas*, but *auctoritas: auctoritas patrum* is the syntagma that defines the specific function of the Senate in the Roman constitution.

In both the history of law and, more generally, philosophy and political theory, all attempts to define this category of *auctoritas*—particularly in contrast to *potestas*—seem to run into almost insurmountable obstacles and aporias. "It is particularly difficult," wrote a French legal historian at the beginning of the 1950s, "to bring the various juridical aspects of the notion of *auctoritas* back to a unitary concept" (Magdelain 1990, 685); and, at the end of that decade, Hannah Arendt could open her essay "What Is Authority?" with the observation that authority had "vanished from the modern world" to such an extent that in the absence of any "authentic and indisputable" experience of it, "the very term has become clouded by controversy and confusion" (Arendt 1961, 91). There is perhaps no better confirmation of this confusion—and of the ambiguities that it entails—than the fact that Arendt undertook her reevaluation of authority only a few years after Adorno and Else Frenkel-Brunswick had conducted their frontal attack on "the authoritarian personality." On the other hand, in forcefully denouncing "the liberal identification of totalitarianism with authoritarianism" (97), Arendt probably did not realize that she shared this denunciation with an author whom she certainly disliked.

Indeed, in 1931, in a book bearing the significant title *Der Hüter der Verfassung* (The guardian of the constitution), Carl Schmitt had tried

to define the president of the Reich's neutral power in the state of exception by dialectically opposing *auctoritas* and *potestas*. After recalling that
both Bodin and Hobbes were still able to appreciate the meaning of the
distinction, Schmitt lamented (in words that anticipate Arendt's argu-
ment) "the lack of tradition of the modern theory of the state, which opposes authority and freedom, authority and democracy . . . to the point
of confusing authority with dictatorship" (Schmitt 1931, 137). Already in
his 1928 treatise on constitutional law, though without defining the opposition, Schmitt evoked its "great importance in the general theory of
the state," and referred back to Roman law to describe it ("the Senate
had *auctoritas;* on the contrary, *potestas* and *imperium* derive from the
people" [Schmitt 1928, 109]).

   In 1968, in a study of the idea of authority published in a *Festgabe* for
Schmitt's eightieth year, a Spanish scholar, Jesus Fueyo, noted that the
modern confusion of *auctoritas* and *potestas* ("two concepts that express
the originary sense through which the Roman people conceived their
communal life" [Fueyo 1968, 213]) and their convergence in the concept
of sovereignty "was the cause of the philosophical inconsistency in the
modern theory of the state"; and he immediately added that this confusion "is not only academic, but is closely bound up with the real process
that has led to the formation of the political order of modernity" (213).
What we must now try to understand is the meaning of this "confusion"
that is bound up with the reflection and political praxis of the West.

א   It is a commonly held opinion that the concept of *auctoritas* is specifically
Roman, just as it is cliché to refer to Dio Cassius in order to demonstrate its un-
translatability into Greek. But despite what is repeatedly claimed, Dio Cassius,
who had an excellent knowledge of Roman law, does not say that the term is impossible to translate; he says, rather, that it cannot be translated *kathapax,* "once
and for all" (*hellēnisai auto kathapax adunaton esti* [*Roman History* 55.3.5]). The
implication here is that it must be rendered in Greek with a different term each
time, depending on the context, which is obvious, given the wide reach of the
concept. What Dio has in mind, therefore, is not something like a Roman specificity of the term but the difficulty of leading it back to a single meaning.

6.2   The definition of the problem is complicated by the fact that the
concept of *auctoritas* refers to a relatively broad juridical phenomenol-

ogy, which concerns both private and public law. It will be best to begin our analysis with the former, and then to see if it is possible to lead the two aspects back to unity.

In the sphere of private law, *auctoritas* is the property of the *auctor*, that is, the person *sui iuris* (the *pater familias*) who intervenes—pronouncing the technical formula *auctor fio* [I am made *auctor*]—in order to confer legal validity on the act of a subject who cannot independently bring a legally valid act into being. Thus, the *auctoritas* of the tutor makes valid the act of one who lacks this capacity, and the *auctoritas* of the father "authorizes"—that is, makes valid—the marriage of the son *in potestate*. Analogously, the seller (in a *mancipatio*) is bound to assist the buyer in confirming his title of ownership in the course of a claim proceeding involving a third opposing party.

The term derives from the verb *augeo*: the *auctor* is *is qui auget*, the person who augments, increases, or perfects the act—or the legal situation—of someone else. In the section of his *Indo-European Language and Society* dedicated to law, Benveniste sought to show that originally the verb *augeo* (which, in the Indo-European area, is significantly related to terms that express force) "denotes not the increase in something which already exists but the act of producing from one's own breast; a creative act" (Benveniste 1969, 2: 148/422). In truth, the two meanings are not contradictory at all in classical law. Indeed, the Greco-Roman world does not know creation *ex nihilo*; rather, every act of creation always involves something else—formless matter or incomplete being—that must be perfected or made to grow. Every creation is always a cocreation, just as every author is always a coauthor. As Magdelain has effectively written, "[A]uctoritas is not sufficient in itself; whether it authorizes or ratifies, it implies an extraneous activity that it validates" (Magdelain 1990, 685). It is, then, as if for something to exist in law there must be a relationship between two elements (or two subjects): one endowed with *auctoritas* and one that takes the initiative in the act in the strict sense. If the two elements or two subjects coincide, then the act is perfect. However, if there is a gap or incongruity between them, the act must be completed with *auctoritas* in order to be valid. But where does the "force" of the *auctor* come from? And what is this power to *augere?*

It has been rightly noted that *auctoritas* has nothing to do with representation, whereby the acts performed by a mandatary or by a legal representative are imputed to the mandator. The *auctor*'s act is not founded upon some sort of legal power vested in him to act as a representative (of the minor or the incompetent): it springs directly from his condition as *pater*. In the same way, the act of the seller, who intervenes as *auctor* to defend the buyer, has nothing to do with a right of guarantee in the modern sense. Pierre Noailles, who had sought in the last years of his life to outline a unitary theory of *auctoritas* in private law, could therefore write that it is "an attribute attached to the person, and originally to the physical person, . . . the privilege, the right that belongs to a Roman, under the required conditions, to serve as a foundation for the legal situation created by others" (Noailles 1948, 274). "Like all the powers of archaic law," he adds, "be they familial, private, or public, *auctoritas* too was originally conceived according to the unilateral model of law pure and simple, without obligation or sanction" (274). And yet we need only reflect on the formula *auctor fio* (and not simply *auctor sum* [I am *auctor*]) to realize that it seems to imply not so much the voluntary exercise of a right as the actualization of an impersonal power [*potenza*] in the very person of the *auctor*.

6.3   As we have seen, in public law *auctoritas* designates the most proper prerogative of the Senate. The active subjects of this prerogative are therefore the *patres: auctoritas patrum* and *patres auctores fiunt* [the fathers are made *auctors*] are common formulas for expressing the constitutional function of the Senate. Legal historians have nevertheless always had difficulty defining this function. Mommsen observed that the Senate does not have an action of its own but can act only in concert with the magistrate or to complete the decisions of popular *comitia* by ratifying laws. The Senate cannot express itself without being questioned by the magistrates and can only request or "counsel"—*consultum* is the technical term—without this "counsel" ever being absolutely binding. The formula of the *senatus consultum* is *si eis videatur*, "if it seems right to them [i.e., the magistrates]"; in the extreme case of the *senatus consultum ultimum*, the formula is slightly more emphatic: *videant consules* [let the consuls see to it]. Mommsen expresses this peculiar character of *auctoritas* when he writes that it is "less than an order and more than a counsel" (Mommsen 1969, 3: 1034).

It is certain, in any case, that *auctoritas* has nothing to do with the *potestas* or the *imperium* of the magistrates or the people. The senator is not a magistrate, and we nearly never find the verb *iubere* [to order], which defines the decisions of the magistrates or the people, used for his "counsels." And yet, with a strong analogy to the figure of the *auctor* in private law, the *auctoritas patrum* intervenes to ratify the decisions of the popular *comitia* and make them fully valid. A single formula *(auctor fio)* designates both the action of the tutor that completes the act of the minor and the senatorial ratification of popular decisions. The analogy here does not necessarily mean that the people must be considered as minors under the tutelage of the *patres;* rather, the essential point is that in this case too there is that duality of elements that in the sphere of private law defines the perfect legal action. *Auctoritas* and *potestas* are clearly distinct, and yet together they form a binary system.

א The polemics among scholars who tend to unify the *auctoritas patrum* and the *auctor* of private law under a single paradigm are easily resolved if one considers that the analogy does not concern the individual figures, but the very structure of the relation between the two elements whose integration constitutes the perfect act. In a study from 1925 that had a strong influence on Roman scholars, Richard Heinze described the common element between the minor and the people with these words: "The minor and the people are determined to bind themselves in a certain direction, but their bond cannot come into being without the collaboration of another subject" (Heinze 1925, 350). That is to say, it is not that scholars tend to "depict public law in the light of private law" (Biscardi 1987, 119), but that there is a structural analogy that, as we will see, concerns the very nature of the law. Juridical validity is not an originary characteristic of human actions but must be conveyed to them through a "power that grants legitimacy" (Magdelain 1990, 686).

6.4   Let us try to better define the nature of this "power that grants legitimacy" in its relation to the *potestas* of the magistrates and the people. What previous attempts to understand this relation have not taken into account is precisely that extreme figure of *auctoritas* that is at issue in the *senatus consultum ultimum* and the *iustitium.* As we have seen,

the *iustitium* produces a true and proper suspension of the juridical order. In particular, the consuls are reduced to the condition of private
citizens *(in privato abditi)*, while every private citizen acts as if he were
invested with an *imperium*. With an inverse symmetry, in 211 BCE, at
Hannibal's approach, a *senatus consultum* resuscitates the *imperium* of
the former dictators, consuls, and censors *(placuit omnes qui dictatores,
consules censoresve fuissent cum imperio esse, donec recessisset a muris
hostis* [It was decreed that all who had been dictators, consuls, or censors should have *imperium*, until the enemy had withdrawn from the
walls] [Livy 26.10.9]). Under extreme conditions (that is to say, under
the conditions that best define it, if it is true that a legal institution's
truest character is always defined by the exception and the extreme situation) *auctoritas* seems to act as *a force that suspends* potestas *where it
took place and reactivates it where it was no longer in force.* It is a power
that suspends or reactivates law, but is not formally in force as law.

This relation—at once one of exclusion and supplementation—
between *auctoritas* and *potestas* is also found in another institution in
which the *auctoritas patrum* once again shows its peculiar function: the
interregnum. Even after the end of the monarchy, when, because of death
or whatever other reason, there remained no consul or other magistrate
in the city (except the representatives of the plebs), the *patres auctores*
(that is, the group of senators who belonged to a consular family, as
opposed to the *patres conscripti* [conscript fathers]) named an *interrex*
who ensured the continuity of power. The formula used was *res publica
ad patres redit* [The republic returns to the fathers] or *auspicia ad patres
redeunt* [The auspices return to the fathers]. As Magdelain has written, "During the *interregnum*, the constitution is suspended. . . . The
Republic is without magistrates, without Senate, without popular assemblies. Then the senatorial group of the *patres* meets, and sovereignly
names the first *interrex*, who in turn sovereignly names his own succes-
sor" (Magdelain 1990, 359–60). Here too, *auctoritas* shows its connection with the suspension of *potestas* and, at the same time, its capacity
to ensure the functioning of the Republic under exceptional circumstances. Once again, this prerogative rests immediately with the *patres
auctores* as such. Indeed, the first *interrex* is not invested with the *imperium* of a magistrate, but solely the *auspicia* (356); and in asserting

against the plebians the importance of the *auspicia,* Appius Claudius states that they belong personally and exclusively to the *patres privatim:* "*nobis adeo propria sunt auspicia, ut . . . privatim auspicia habeamus* [The auspices belong so properly to us that . . . we have them as private citizens]" (Livy 6.41.6). The power to reactivate vacant *potestas* is not a legal power received from the people or a magistrate but springs immediately from the personal condition of the *patres.*

6.5   A third institution in which *auctoritas* shows its specific function of suspending law is the *hostis iudicatio.* In exceptional situations where a Roman citizen threatened the security of the Republic by conspiracy or treason, he could be declared *hostis,* "public enemy," by the Senate. The *hostis iudicatus* was not simply likened to a foreign enemy, the *hostis alienigena,* because the latter was always protected by the *ius gentium* [law of peoples] (Nissen 1877, 27); he was, rather, radically deprived of any legal status and could therefore be stripped of his belongings and put to death at any moment. What *auctoritas* suspends here is not simply the juridical order, but the *ius civis,* the very status of the Roman citizen.

The relation—at once antagonistic and supplementary—between *auctoritas* and *potestas* is finally shown in a terminological peculiarity that Mommsen was the first to notice. The syntagma *senatus auctoritas* is used in a technical sense to designate a *senatus consultum* that, because it has been opposed by an *intercessio,* is without legal effects and can therefore not be executed (even if it was entered as such among the official acts, *auctoritas perscripta*). That is, the *auctoritas* of the Senate appears in its purest and most perspicuous form when it has been invalidated by the *potestas* of a magistrate, when it lives as mere writing in absolute opposition to the law's being in force [*vigenza*]. For a moment here *auctoritas* shows its essence: the power [*potenza*] that can at once "grant legitimacy" and suspend law exhibits its most proper character at the point of its greatest legal inefficacy. It is what remains of law if law is wholly suspended (in this sense, in Benjamin's reading of Kafka's allegory, not law but life—law that blurs at every point with life).

6.6   It is perhaps in the *auctoritas principis*—that is, in the moment when Augustus, in a famous passage of the *Res gestae,* claims *auctori-*

tas as the foundation of his status as *princeps*—that we can better understand the meaning of this unique prerogative. It is significant that the rebirth of modern studies of *auctoritas* coincides precisely with the publication in 1924 of the *Monumentum Antiochenum,* which allowed a more accurate reconstruction of the passage in question. The issue here concerned a series of fragments of a Latin inscription containing a passage from chapter 34 of the *Res gestae,* which was extant in its entirety only in the Greek version. Mommsen had reconstructed the Latin text in these terms: "*post id tempus praestiti omnibus dignitate* (axiōmati), *potestatis autem nihil amplius habui quam qui fuerunt mihi quoque in magistratu conlegae* [After that time I surpassed all in *dignitas,* although I had no more *potestas* than those who were my colleagues in each magistracy]." The Antiochean inscription showed that Augustus had written not *dignitate* but *auctoritate.* Commenting in 1925 on the new information, Heinze wrote, "We philologists should all be ashamed for having blindly followed Mommsen's authority: the only possible antithesis to *potestas*—that is, to the legal power of a magistrate—was, in this passage, not *dignitas,* but *auctoritas*" (Heinze 1925, 348).

As often happens—and, moreover, as scholars did not fail to observe—the rediscovery of the concept (no fewer than fifteen important monographs on *auctoritas* appeared in the following ten years) kept pace with the growing weight that the authoritarian principle was assuming in the political life of European societies. "*Auctoritas,*" wrote a German scholar in 1937, "that is, the fundamental concept of public law in our modern authoritarian states, can only be understood—not only literally but also as regards the content—starting from Roman law of the time of the principate" (Wenger 1939, 152). And yet it is possible that this nexus between Roman law and our own political experience is precisely what still remains for us to investigate.

6.7   If we now return to the passage from the *Res gestae,* the decisive point is that here Augustus defines the specificity of his constitutional power not in the certain terms of a *potestas,* which he says he shares with those who are his colleagues in the magistracy, but in the vaguer terms of an *auctoritas.* The meaning of the name "Augustus," which the Senate conferred on him on January 16, 27 BCE, accords entirely with this claim: it comes from the same root as *augeo* and *auctor* and, as Dio Cassius notes, "does not mean a *potestas* [*dunamis*] . . . but shows the splendor of *auctoritas* [*tēn tou axiōmatos lamprotēta*]" (*Roman History* 53.18.2).

In the edict of January 13 of the same year, in which he declares his intention to restore the republican constitution, Augustus defines himself as *optimi status auctor* [*auctor* of the highest standing]. As Magdelain has acutely observed, the term *auctor* here does not have the generic meaning of "founder," but the technical meaning of "guarantor in a *mancipatio*." Because Augustus conceives of the restoration of the Republic as a transfer of the *res publica* from his hands to those of the people and the Senate (see *Res gestae* 34.1), it is possible that "in the formula *auctor optimi status* . . . the term *auctor* has a rather precise legal meaning and refers to the idea of the transfer of the *res publica*. . . . Augustus would thus be the *auctor* of the rights rendered to the people and the Senate, just as, in a mancipation, the *mancipio dans* is the *auctor* of the power acquired by the *mancipio accipiens* over the transferred object" (Magdelain 1947, 57).

In any case, the Roman principate—which we are used to describing with a term (emperor) that refers back to the *imperium* of the magistrate—is not a magistracy, but an extreme form of *auctoritas*. Heinze has described this contrast perfectly: "Every magistracy is a preestablished form, which the individual enters into and which constitutes the source of his power; *auctoritas*, on the other hand, springs from the person, as something that is constituted through him, lives only in him, and disappears with him" (Heinze 1925, 356). Though Augustus receives all magistracies from the people and the Senate, *auctoritas* is instead bound to his person and constitutes him as *auctor optimi status*, as he who legitimates and guarantees the whole of Roman political life.

Hence the peculiar status of his person, which manifests itself in a fact whose importance has not yet been fully appreciated by scholars. Dio Cassius informs us that Augustus "made all of his house public [*tēn oikian edēmosiōse pasan*] . . . so as to live at once in public and in private [*hin' en tois idiois hama kai en tois koinois oikoiē*]" (*Roman History* 55.12.5). It is the *auctoritas* that he embodies, and not the magistracies with which he has been invested, that make it impossible to isolate in him something like a private life and *domus*. This is also the sense in which one must interpret the fact that a *signum* to Vesta is dedicated in the house of Augustus on the Palatine. Fraschetti has rightly observed that, given the close connection between the cult of Vesta and the cult of the public Penates of the Roman people, this meant that the Penates of Augustus's family were identified with those of the Roman people and that therefore "the private cults of a family . . . and preeminently communal cults in the sphere of the city (those of Vesta and the public Penates of the Roman people) would seem in fact to become homologous in the house of Augustus" (Fraschetti 1990, 359). Unlike the life of the common citizens, the "august" life can no longer be defined through the opposition of public and private.

℘ It is in this light that Kantorowicz's theory of the king's two bodies should be reread, so that we can make some refinements to it. Kantorowicz (who generally undervalues the importance of the Roman precedent to the theory that he seeks to reconstruct for the English and French monarchies) does not relate the distinction between *auctoritas* and *potestas* to the problem of the king's two bodies and the principle *dignitas non moritur* [*dignitas* does not die]. And yet it is precisely because the sovereign was first and foremost the embodiment of an *auctoritas*, and not solely of a *potestas*, that *auctoritas* was so closely bound to his physical person, thus requiring the complicated ritual of constructing a wax double of the sovereign in the *funus imaginarium*. The end of a magistracy as such does not entail a problem of bodies at all: One magistrate succeeds another without having to presuppose the immortality of the office. Only because, from the Roman *princeps* on, the sovereign expresses an *auctoritas* in his very person, only because in "august" life public and private have entered into a zone of absolute indistinction, does it becomes necessary to distinguish two bodies in order to ensure the continuity of *dignitas* (which is simply a synonym for *auctoritas*).

To understand modern phenomena such as the Fascist *Duce* and the Nazi *Führer*, it is important not to forget their continuity with the principle of the *auctoritas principis*. As we have already observed, even though Mussolini held the office of head of the government and Hitler that of chancellor of the Reich (just as Augustus held *imperium consolare* or *potestas tribunica*) neither the *Duce* nor the *Führer* represents a constitutionally defined public office or magistracy. The qualities of *Duce* or *Führer* are immediately bound to the physical person and belong to the biopolitical tradition of *auctoritas* and not to the legal tradition of *potestas.*

6.8   It is significant that modern scholars have been so ready to uphold the claim that *auctoritas* inheres immediately in the living person of the *pater* or the *princeps.* What was clearly an ideology or a *fictio* intended to ground the preeminence or, in any case, the specific rank of *auctoritas* in relation to *potestas* thus becomes a figure of law's immanence to life. It is not by chance that this should happen precisely in the years when the authoritarian principle saw an unexpected rebirth in Europe through fascism and National Socialism. Though it was obvious that there cannot be some sort of eternal human type periodically embodied in Augustus, Napoleon, or Hitler, and that there are only more or less similar legal apparatuses (the state of exception, the *iustitium,* the *auctoritas principis, Führertum*) that are put to use under more or less different circumstances, the power that Weber called "charismatic" was nevertheless linked in 1930s Germany (and elsewhere) to the concept of *auctoritas* and elaborated in a theory of *Führertum* as the originary and personal power of a leader. Thus in 1933, in a short article that seeks to outline the fundamental concepts of National Socialism, Schmitt defines the principle of *Führung* through "the ancestral identity between leader and followers" (note the use of Weberian concepts). 1938 saw the publication of the Berlin jurist Heinrich Triepel's book *Die Hegemonie,* which Schmitt quickly reviewed. In its first section, the book expounds a theory of *Führertum* as an authority founded not on a preexisting order but on a personal charisma. The *Führer* is defined through psychological categories (energetic, conscious, and creative will), and his unity with the social group and the originary and personal character of his power are strongly underscored.

Then in 1947, the elderly Roman scholar Pietro De Francisci published *Arcana imperii,* in which he dedicates a good deal of space to an analysis of the "primary type" of power that he (seeking to distance himself from fascism with a sort of euphemism) defines as *ductus* (and the leader in which it is embodied as *ductor*). De Francisci transforms the Weberian tripartition of power (traditional, legal, charismatic) into a dichotomy drawn on the opposition of authority and power [*potestà*]. The authority of the *ductor* or the *Führer* can never be derivative but is always originary and springs from his person; furthermore, in its essence it is not coercive, but is rather founded, as Triepel had already shown, on consent and the free acknowledgment of a "superiority of value."

Though both Triepel and De Francisci had fascist and Nazi techniques of government before their eyes, neither appears to have been aware that the power they describe attains its appearance of originality from the suspension or neutralization of the juridical order—that is, ultimately, from the state of exception. "Charisma"—as its reference to Paul's *kharis* [grace] (which Weber knew perfectly well) could have suggested—coincides with the neutralization of law and not with a more originary figure of power.

In each case, what the three authors seem to take for granted is that authoritarian-charismatic power springs almost magically from the very person of the *Führer*. Law's claim that it coincides at an eminent point with life could not have been affirmed more forcefully. In this regard, the theory of *auctoritas* converged at least in part with the tradition of juridical thought that saw law as ultimately identical with—or immediately articulated to—life. Savigny's maxim ("Law is nothing but life considered from a particular point of view") finds a counterpart in the twentieth century in Rudolph Smend's thesis that "the norm receives the grounds of its validity [*Geltungsgrund*], the quality of its validity, and the content of its validity from life and the sense attributed to it, just as, inversely, life must be understood only in relation to its assigned and regulated vital sense [*Lebenssinn*]" (Smend 1956, 300). Just as, in Romantic ideology, something like a language became fully comprehensible only in its immediate relation to a people (and vice versa), so law and life must be tightly implicated in a reciprocal grounding. The dialectic of *auctoritas* and *potestas* expressed precisely this implication (and in this sense, one can speak of an originary biopolitical character of the paradigm of *auctoritas*). The norm can be applied to the normal situation and can be suspended without totally annulling the juridical order because in the form of *auctoritas*, or sovereign decision, it refers immediately to life, it springs from life.

6.9   It is perhaps possible at this point to look back upon the path traveled thus far and draw some provisional conclusions from our investigation of the state of exception. The juridical system of the West appears as a double structure, formed by two heterogeneous yet coordinated elements: one that is normative and juridical in the strict sense (which we can for convenience inscribe under the rubric *potestas*) and one that is anomic and metajuridical (which we can call by the name *auctoritas*).

The normative element needs the anomic element in order to be applied, but, on the other hand, *auctoritas* can assert itself only in the validation or suspension of *potestas*. Because it results from the dialectic between these two somewhat antagonistic yet functionally connected elements, the ancient dwelling of law is fragile and, in straining to maintain its own order, is always already in the process of ruin and decay. The state of exception is the device that must ultimately articulate and hold together the two aspects of the juridico-political machine by instituting a threshold of undecidability between anomie and *nomos*, between life and law, between *auctoritas* and *potestas*. It is founded on the essential fiction according to which anomie (in the form of *auctoritas*, living law, or the force of law) is still related to the juridical order and the power to suspend the norm has an immediate hold on life. As long as the two elements remain correlated yet conceptually, temporally, and subjectively distinct (as in republican Rome's contrast between the Senate and the people, or in medieval Europe's contrast between spiritual and temporal powers) their dialectic—though founded on a fiction—can nevertheless function in some way. But when they tend to coincide in a single person, when the state of exception, in which they are bound and blurred together, becomes the rule, then the juridico-political system transforms itself into a killing machine.

6.10   The aim of this investigation—in the urgency of the state of exception "in which we live"—was to bring to light the fiction that governs this *arcanum imperii* [secret of power] par excellence of our time. What the "ark" of power contains at its center is the state of exception—but this is essentially an empty space, in which a human action with no relation to law stands before a norm with no relation to life.

This does not mean that the machine, with its empty center, is not effective; on the contrary, what we have sought to show is precisely that it has continued to function almost without interruption from World War One, through fascism and National Socialism, and up to our own time. Indeed, the state of exception has today reached its maximum worldwide deployment. The normative aspect of law can thus be obliterated and contradicted with impunity by a governmental violence that— while ignoring international law externally and producing a permanent state of exception internally—nevertheless still claims to be applying the law.

Of course, the task at hand is not to bring the state of exception back within its spatially and temporally defined boundaries in order to then reaffirm the primacy of a norm and of rights that are themselves ultimately grounded in it. From the real state of exception in which we live, it is not possible to return to the state of law [*stato di diritto*], for at issue now are the very concepts of "state" and "law." But if it is possible to attempt to halt the machine, to show its central fiction, this is because between violence and law, between life and norm, there is no substantial articulation. Alongside the movement that seeks to keep them in relation at all costs, there is a countermovement that, working in an inverse direction in law and in life, always seeks to loosen what has been artificially and violently linked. That is to say, in the field of tension of our culture, two opposite forces act, one that institutes and makes, and one that deactivates and deposes. The state of exception is both the point of their maximum tension and—as it coincides with the rule—that which threatens today to render them indiscernible. To live in the state of exception means to experience both of these possibilities and yet, by always separating the two forces, ceaselessly to try to interrupt the working of the machine that is leading the West toward global civil war.

6.11   If it is true that the articulation between life and law, between anomie and *nomos,* that is produced by the state of exception is effective though fictional, one can still not conclude from this that somewhere either beyond or before juridical apparatuses there is an immediate access to something whose fracture and impossible unification are represented by these apparatuses. There are not *first* life as a natural biological given and anomie as the state of nature, and *then* their implication in law through the state of exception. On the contrary, the very possibility of distinguishing life and law, anomie and *nomos,* coincides with their articulation in the biopolitical machine. Bare life is a product of the machine and not something that preexists it, just as law has no court in nature or in the divine mind. Life and law, anomie and *nomos, auctoritas* and *potestas,* result from the fracture of something to which we have no other access than through the fiction of their articulation and the patient work that, by unmasking this fiction, separates what it had claimed to unite. But disenchantment does not restore the enchanted thing to its original state: According to the principle that purity never lies at the origin, disenchantment gives it only the possibility of reaching a new condition.

To show law in its nonrelation to life and life in its nonrelation to law means to open a space between them for human action, which once claimed for itself the name of "politics." Politics has suffered a lasting eclipse because it has been contaminated by law, seeing itself, at best, as constituent power (that is, violence that makes law), when it is not reduced to merely the power to negotiate with the law. The only truly political action, however, is that which severs the nexus between violence and law. And only beginning from the space thus opened will it be possible to pose the question of a possible use of law after the deactivation of the device that, in the state of exception, tied it to life. We will then have before us a "pure" law, in the sense in which Benjamin speaks of a "pure" language and a "pure" violence. To a word that does not bind, that neither commands nor prohibits anything, but says only itself, would correspond an action as pure means, which shows only itself, without any relation to an end. And, between the two, not a lost original state, but only the use and human praxis that the powers of law and myth had sought to capture in the state of exception.

References

Arangio-Ruiz, Gaetano. 1913. *Istituzioni di diritto costituzionale italiano.* Reprint, Milan: Bocca, 1972.

Arendt, Hannah. 1961. *Between Past and Future.* New York: Viking.

Balladore-Pallieri, Giorgio. 1970. *Diritto costituzionale.* Milan: Giuffrè.

Bengel, Johann Albrecht. 1734. *Vorrede zur Handausgabe des griechischen N. T.*

Benjamin, Walter. 1921. Zur Kritik der Gewalt. In Tiedemann and Schweppenhäuser, *Gesammelte Schriften,* vol. 2, pt. 1. Translated by Edmund Jephcott as Critique of violence. In *Selected Writings,* vol. 1, *1913–1926,* ed. Marcus Bullock and Michael W. Jennings. Cambridge: Harvard University Press, Belknap Press, 1996.

———. 1928. *Ursprung des deutschen Trauerspiels.* In Tiedemann and Schweppenhäuser, *Gesammelte Schriften,* vol. 1, pt. 1. Translated by John Osborne as *The Origin of German Tragic Drama.* London: Verso, 1998.

———. 1931. Karl Kraus. In Tiedemann and Schweppenhäuser, *Gesammelte Schriften,* vol. 2, pt. 1. Translated by Edmund Jephcott as Karl Kraus. In *Selected Writings,* vol. 2, *1927–1934,* ed. Michael W. Jennings, Howard Eiland, and Gary Smith. Cambridge: Harvard University Press, Belknap Press, 1999.

———. 1934. Franz Kafka. In Tiedemann and Schweppenhäuser, *Gesammelte Schriften,* vol. 2, pt. 2. Translated by Harry Zohn as Franz Kafka. In *Selected Writings,* vol. 2, ed. Michael W. Jennings, Howard Eiland, and Gary Smith. Cambridge: Harvard University Press, Belknap Press, 1999.

———. 1942. Über den Begriff der Geschichte. In Tiedemann and Schweppenhäuser, *Gesammelte Schriften,* vol. 1, pt. 2. Translated by Harry Zohn as On the concept of history. In *Selected Writings,* vol. 4, *1938–1940,* ed. Howard Eiland and Michael W. Jennings. Cambridge: Harvard University Press, Belknap Press, 2003.

———. 1966. *Breife.* 2 vols. Ed. Gershom Scholem and Theodor W. Adorno. Frankfurt am Main: Suhrkamp. Translated by Manfred R. Jacobson and Evelyn M. Jacobson as *The Correspondence of Walter Benjamin,* ed. Gershom Scholem and Theodor W. Adorno. Chicago: University of Chicago Press, 1994.

———. 1972–89. *Gesammelte Schriften.* 7 vols. Ed. Rolf Tiedemann and Hermann Schweppenhäuser. Frankfurt am Main: Suhrkamp.

———. 1992. Notizen zu einer Arbeit über die Kategorie der Gerechtigkeit. *Frankfurter Adorno Blätter 4.*

Benveniste, Émile. 1969. *Le Vocabulaire des institutions indo-européennes.* 2 vols. Paris: Minuit. Translated by Elizabeth Palmer as *Indo-European Language and Society.* Coral Gables, FL: University of Miami Press, 1973.

Biscardi, Arnaldo. 1987. *Autoritas patrum: Problemi di storia del diritto pubblico romano.* Naples: Jovene.

Bredekamp, Horst. 1998. Von W. Benjamin zu C. Schmitt. *Deutsche Zeitschrift für Philosophie* 46.

Delatte, Armand. 1922. *Essai sur la politique pythagoricienne.* Paris: Champion.

Delatte, Louis. 1942. *Les traités de la royauté d'Ecphante, Diotogène et Sthénidas.* Paris: Droz.

De Martino, Francesco. 1973. *Storia della costituzione romana.* Naples: Jovene.

Derrida, Jacques. 1994. *Force de loi.* Paris: Galilée. Translated by Mary Quaintance as Force of law: The "mystical foundation of authority." *Cardozo Law Review* 11, nos. 5–6 (1990).

Drobische, Klaus, and Günther Wieland. 1993. *System der NS-Konzentrationslager 1933–1939.* Berlin: Akademie.

Duguit, Léon. 1930. *Traité de droit constitutionnel.* Vol. 3. Paris: de Boccard.

Durkheim, Émile. 1897. *Le Suicide. Étude de sociologie.* Paris: Alcan. Translated by John A. Spaulding and George Simpson as *Suicide: A Study in Sociology.* New York: Free Press, 1951.

Ehrenberg, Victor. 1924. Monumentum Antiochenum. *Klio* 19.

Fontana, Alessandro. 1999. Du droit de résistance au devoir d'insurrection. In *Le droit de résistance,* ed. Jean-Claude Zancarini. Paris: ENS.

Fraschetti, Augusto. 1990. *Roma e il principe.* Rome-Bari: Laterza.

Fresa, Carlo. 1981. *Provvisorietà con forza di legge e gestione degli stati di crisi.* Padua: CEDAM.

Friedrich, Carl J. [1941] 1950. *Constitutional Government and Democracy.* 2nd. ed. Boston: Ginn.

Fueyo, Jesus. 1968. Die Idee des "Auctoritas": Genesis und Entwicklung. In *Epirrrhosis. Festgabe für Carl Schmitt,* ed. Hans Barion. Berlin: Duncker & Humblot.

Gadamer, Hans-Georg, 1960. *Wahrheit und Methode.* Tübingen: Mohr. Translated by Joel Weinsheimer and Donald Marshall as *Truth and Method.* 2d rev. ed. New York: Crossroads, 1989.

Hatschek, Julius. 1923. *Deutsches und Preussisches Staatsrecht.* Vol. 2. Berlin: Stilke.

Heinze, Richard. 1925. Auctoritas. *Hermes* 60.

Kohler, Josef. 1915. *Not kennt kein Gebot.* Berlin-Leipzig: Rothschild.

Magdelain, André. 1947. *Auctoritas principis.* Paris: Belles Letters.

———. 1990. *Ius Imperium Auctoritas. Études de droit romain.* Rome: École française de Rome.

Mathiot, André. 1956. La théorie des circonstances exceptionelles. In *Mélanges Mestre.* Paris: n.p.

Meuli, Karl. 1975. *Gesammelte Schriften.* 2 vols. Basel-Stuttgart: Schwabe.

Middell, Emil. 1887. *De iustitio deque aliis quibusdam iuris publici romani notionibus.* Minden, Germany: Bruns.

Mommsen, Theodor. 1969. *Römisches Staatsrecht.* 3 vols. Reprint, Graz: Akademische Druck. Orig. pub. 1871.

Nissen, Adolph. 1877. *Das Iustitium. Eine Studie aus der römischen Rechtsgeschichte.* Leipzig: Gebhardt.

Noailles, Pierre. 1948. *Fas et Ius. Études de droit romain.* Paris: Belles Lettres.

Plaumann, Gerhard. 1913. Das sogennante Senatus consultum ultimum, die Quasidiktatur der späteren römischen Republik. *Klio* 13.

Quadri, Giovanni. 1979. *La forza di legge.* Milan: Giuffrè.

Reinach, Theodor. 1885. *De l'etat de siège. Étude historique et juridique.* Paris: Pichon.

Romano, Santi. 1909. Sui decreti-legge e lo stato di assedio in occasione dei terremoti di Messina e Reggio Calabria. In *Scritti minori.* Vol. 1. Reprint, Milan: Giuffrè, 1990.

———. 1983. *Frammenti di un dizionario giuridico.* Milan: Giuffrè.

Roosevelt, Franklin D. 1938. *The Public Papers and Addresses.* Vol. 2. New York: Random House.

Rossiter, Clinton L. 1948. *Constitutional Dictatorship: Crisis Government in the Modern Democracies.* New York: Harcourt Brace.

Saint-Bonnet, François. 2001. *L'état d'exception.* Paris: Presses Universitaires de France.

Schmitt, Carl. 1921. *Die Diktatur.* Munich-Leipzig: Duncker & Humblot.

———. 1922. *Politische Theologie.* Munich-Leipzig: Duncker & Humblot; Translated by George Schwab as *Political Theology.* Cambridge: MIT Press, 1985.

———. 1928. *Verfassungslehre.* Munich-Leipzig: Duncker & Humblot.

———. 1931. *Der Hüter der Verfassung.* Tübingen: Mohr.

———. 1995. *Staat, Großraum, Nomos.* Berlin: Duncker & Humblot.

Schnur, Roman. 1983. *Revolution und Weltbürgerkrieg.* Berlin: Duncker & Humblot.

Schütz, Anton. 1995. L'immaculée conception de l'interprète et l'émergence du système juridique: À propos de fiction et construction en droit. *Droits* 21.

Seston, William. 1962. Les chevaliers romains et le *iustitium* de Germanicus. In *Scripta varia.* Reprint, Rome: École française de Rome, 1980.

Smend, Rudolph. 1956. Integrationslehre. In *Handwörterbuch der Sozialwissenschaften.* Vol. 5. Stuttgart: Fischer; Tübingen: Mohr; Göttingen: Vandenhoeck & Ruprecht.

Taubes, Jacob. 1987. *Ad Carl Schmitt. Gegenstrebige Fügung.* Berlin: Merve.

Tingsten, Herbert. 1934. *Les pleins pouvoirs. L'expansion des pouvoirs gouvernementaux pendant et après la grande guerre.* Paris: Stock.

Versnel, H. S. 1980. Destruction, *devotio,* and despair in a situation of anomy: The mourning for Germanicus in triple perspective. In *Perennitas. Studi in onore di Angelo Brelich.* Rome: Edizioni dell'Ateneo.

Viesel, Hansjörg. 1988. *Jawohl, der Schmitt. Zehn Briefe aus Plettenberg.* Berlin: Support.

Wagenvoort, H. 1947. *Roman Dynamism.* Oxford: Blackwell.

Watkins, Frederick M. 1940. The Problem of Constitutional Dictatorship. *Public Policy* 1.

Weber, Samuel. 1992. Taking exception to decision: W. Benjamin and C. Schmitt. In *Walter Benjamin,* ed. Uwe Steiner. Bern: Lang.

Wenger, Leopold. 1939. Römisches Recht in Amerika. In *Studi di storia e diritto in onore di Enrico Besta.* Vol. 1. Milan: Giuffrè.

Index

94   Index